THE TALE OF CELLAR CAT AND BUG

BY

D1528995

H. C. RABBIT

Cover art by Michelle Savoia

Table of Contents

CELLAR CAT 3

BUG 5

A NEW FRIEND 11

KITTEN 20

A BLUSTERY DAY 22

BIG NEWS 27

GONE..39

SURRENDERED...43

HOMECOMING..45

THE CRATE..52

FORGIVENESS...60

MAINE...67

SEA CAT 73

A BULLY..102

BABIES...141

BYE BUG 177

TEMPLETON ESQUIRE 216

CELLAR CAT

Beyond the bustling city center and past the clustered walkways with throngs of foggy city dwellers and doe-eyed tourists, rests a sleepy three-block neighborhood. Flowering trees and lamp-posts dot the brick-laid sidewalks. Tucked within the trimmed hedges stands a row of dusty red brownstones, all with matching powder blue doors and window boxes. Every spring, each window overflows with a variety of pastel perennials.

One of the blue doors has a brass cat door knocker. It's through this door and in this brownstone that a black-and-white cat lives and because she resides in the cellar, she is named Cellar Cat.

But it isn't an ordinary mildew cement basement. When the cat was young, the floor was lush with wall-to-wall spongy gray carpet. A doughy sofa sat in the center of the room with two plump red armchairs on either end. Black kittens in red bow ties pranced across white wallpaper.

The basement was cozy in the winter and cool in the summer. This, to the cat, was a paradise.

She had access to the main floor through a pet flap in the door at the top of the stairs. Once a day the cat would scale the stairs, climb through the flap and eat a meal laid out for her. She would meow a quick hello, thank you, and goodbye to her owners before slinking back downstairs to her beloved basement. The rest of her day consisted of napping, lazy play, deep stretches, and more napping. She was as happy as a cat could be in her quiet, comfortable home. However, change can happen when you least expect it, and for Cellar Cat, the unexpected was noisily snoring at a shelter downtown.

BUG

Spring had sprung. The window boxes were bursting with flowering pastels. A robin chirped from the blossoming branch of a cherry tree.

Cellar Cat was busy sleeping on the sofa when the basement door opened, followed by footsteps down the staircase. This was odd because the owners rarely ventured below the main floor. More curious was when she raised her head, she saw the woman carrying a heaping white bundle. This piqued her interest. Surely it was a new bed or toy. The cat was always up for a gift.

The man and woman paused at the bottom step, where the woman carefully placed the bundle on the carpet.

"Kitty, come see what we've brought you," she said.

As it would not do to seem overly enthusiastic, the cat had a thorough yawn and leisurely stretch before slipping down to investigate. When she approached the heap, it moved. She jumped; fur raised. What's this? she wondered. A black nose and two wide eyes peeked over the slouchy back end. A dog! A stinking dog!

She sniffed. Not a pleasant odor. It smelled of overripe cheese and sour cabbage. She turned up her nose with a snort and clambered back onto the sofa.

The cat aimlessly batted a mouse toy, then curled up to resume her nap, feeling secure with the knowledge that if she rejected the thing, it would be taken away.

"Don't be that way. We've got you a new friend," the woman said. Cellar Cat ignored her, turning her back to the dog. "You must be lonely down here by yourself."

The woman spoke softly. The cat swatted at the toy mouse with force.

The man kneeled, his tone both kind and firm.

"His name is Bug. He's a good boy, and you'll be best buds in no time. You'll see."

"Not going to happen," she meowed in response.

The man, not fluent in cat speak, was satisfied that the two would work it out. He patted her head, took the woman's hand and walked back upstairs. Once the door closed, Cellar Cat turned, expecting to see an empty spot where the dog had been. To her surprise there he sat like a lumpy white cushion. His round inquisitive face watched her with interest.

She yawned.

"Dog, go away." She extended her claws menacingly in his direction, hoping he took it as a threat. She then pretended to rest. Facing away from Bug, she kept an ear to him. Dogs weren't to be trusted. Her mom told her that.

"If that's your wish, lady." he said. The cat lifted her head regally.

"It is."

With sloth-like speed, he got to his feet and without taking his attention off the cat, lumbered to the opposite corner of the room. His tail wagged intermittently as if expecting a kind gesture. Perhaps, he anticipated she might change her mind and invite him in for a snuggle. No such luck.

"And stop staring at me," she spit. She had met very few animals and thought this one to be overly-friendly. What was the tail wagging about? They didn't know each other.

"Oh, I'm sorry." He looked to the floor. "It's just that I've never seen a feline quite like you before." When he raised his chin, his cheeks were pink. "And what an impressive tail."

Her tail was magnificent. It was a little longer than average with a plumage of fluffy black and white fur. "True." She groomed it to emphasize its beauty.

"You've seen many cats then?"

"Yeah, at the shelter. I was there for a long time because I'm old." He paused to rub his rear on the corner of an old dresser. "There were plenty of cats and kittens, but none as unique."

"I am special. The owners say so." She thought it odd a dog would complement her as she was under the impression that it was in a dog's nature to hate cats and vice versa.

Was it normal for one to compliment another at the first meeting? Or to be desperate for attention? The dog was annoying, but he seemed harmless enough and did know how to pay a compliment, which could come in handy on those feeling-bad-about-yourself kinds of days.

He was pitiful, sitting there sad-like in the corner.

Cellar Cat batted the toy mouse in his direction. It landed at his feet. "You may stay for now but eyes elsewhere." She swished her glorious tail. It was temporary after all. Soon it would be too crowded for him.

"Of course, lady."

"That's another thing," she said. 'my name is Cellar Cat, and I am no lady. I'd appreciate you not referring to me as inferior as a human." Her voice was sharp. "I'm a cat!"
"Understood." He gave a deep bow. "I'm Bug, by the..."
"Yes, yes." She gave a royal wave. "Go!"

A NEW FRIEND

The next weeks were trying for Cellar Cat. Though the dog had a thorough bath and smelled considerably better, his intrusion was almost more than she could bear. The basement walls and those prancing kittens were closing in on her. Once a paradise, the basement now felt like a prison. Although Bug made frequent visits to the main floor, he spent most of his time downstairs flinging his dumb dog toys about and smiling. Her biggest pet peeves about Bug were as follows:

He took too long to think before he spoke.

He dragged out his words.

He gave out boring, unsolicited advice.

The dog was also slow-moving, thoughtful, and patient. Characteristics the feline found insufferable. She once compared him to a tortoise. To which he replied, "Surely, I'm not that handsome."

It was as if no insult bothered him. After much trial and error, she did find one diss that had the desired effect: calling him Bozo. He visibly bristled at the name, therefore, she used it often. The two roomies had little in common. For instance, Cellar Cat despised the outdoors, while Bug delighted in it. At the dark end of the basement was a doggie door that led to the backyard. The property was protected by a wrought-iron fence. Guarding the entrance was a double-latched metal gate sculpted with painted white swans.

Bug routinely took walks around the enclosure. Beginning in the garden, he'd sniff around the many lilac bushes that dotted the perimeter then kindly plod through the weeds surrounding the owner's prized geraniums. From there, he'd waddle breathless into the rear herb garden, all the while seeking out new friends and experiences. From her basement window seat, Cellar Cat would watch him with an air of contempt.

The ease at which he came and went bothered her. Many times, he invited her to join him but, with a tense brow, she refused.

"No thank you, Bozo." She'd say.

She knew too well that nothing good came from going outdoors. More importantly, she had to stay watchful and alert. Being outside could prove too great a distraction.

"I met someone extraordinary today." Bug said one morning after his walk.

"Not interested." Cellar Cat was grooming herself on the sofa.

"If you met him you wouldn't say that. What an interesting fellow."

She blinked hard and yawned big.

"Fine. What's this fellow's name?"

"I'm not sure. I call him Squirrelly." He scratched his chin with his front paw. "Because he's a squirrel."

"Wow." She extended her back in a deep stretch then snickered, "Here's my input. One-he's a squirrel, maybe you should have higher standards. Two- you don't know his name, so you just give him a one, and three- the name you chose is Squirrelly? Real original, Bozo."

Bug's jaw clenched, then he laughed. "Yeah, I guess I could have thought of a better name. But I don't speak squirrel. I'm certain that's what he mimed to me and I had to address him as something."

He itched his belly with his back foot.

"He's a hard worker. He told me that all day every day he seeks out and stores nuts, always hiding them in different locations to mislead other squirrels."

"Huh? You got all that without understanding squirrel?"

"I recognize a few words. Mostly I watch his body language. I put the two together and have a basic understanding." He plopped down thoughtfully, one paw over the other. "Squirrelly also gathers intel from all three blocks and even farther! Imagine that. He's really got his vestigial thumb on the pulse of the neighborhood."

"Whoop-de-do! The neighborhood, you say? I'm sure the lives of everyone on these three blocks depend on him." She chuckled, primping her tail.

"Umm, it could. There's an underground network, literally. Moles, rabbits and opossums are informants. Just the other day he was tipped off by a chipmunk that there was a rat in apartment building 1423, room eight."

Cellar Cat's body stiffened. She detested rodents. "Ok, I'll bite. Do tell."

Bug watched a fly land on his nose, chortled, then gently shooed it away. "It turned out to be stuffed. But..."
"Oh!" she cried, shaking her head.
"It could easily have been a real one. Think about it. We would've had an infestation on our hands."
Cellar Cat shifted her body and resumed cleaning. Bug found a dust bunny. He alternated sucking his breath in to pull it toward him and blowing out to send it away.

"Anyway, he has an issue with a squirrel that steals his nuts. I told him to bury stones. While the other squirrel is busy digging those up, Squirrelly could bury the real ones. He appreciated my advice and offered me a peanut, which in the squirrel world is a pretty big deal." Under the belief that Bug had a slow mind, the cat was taken aback by his problem-solving skills.

He stood up and rubbed his hip on the sofa leg jostling it and disturbing Cellar Cat's bath. Unaware of the nasty look she gave him, he continued.

"I declined of course 'cause I don't eat nuts. Indigestion, you know."

Annoyed by his rude sofa-wriggling, she said, "Hmmm, I was thinking, Bozo, about hunting that very same squirrel." She lifted the side of her lip to reveal a single sparkling fang.

Bug's face fell.

"Not kill him or anything. No, no." She stood and leered down at him. "Just an appreciation-of-life kind of chase. Maybe whack him around a bit. Nothing more."

The dog sank to the floor. The cat raised a brow. "I'll have to revisit that idea."

Bug's mouth drooped. "You wouldn't. Not Squirrelly." He tried to rise in protest but his stiff joints slowed him.

"Woah, don't get your dander up, Shorty," Cellar Cat snickered.

She stretched, eyeing her toy mouse beside one of the red chairs.

"Look, as much as I've enjoyed your rundown of the day's event, it's my playtime. Must keep those skills sharp for squirrels—or an infestation of stuffed rats." She shooed him aside. "Now, be gone, slow one."

Bug sagged. "Alright." he headed for the stairs.

"But you won't hurt him?" Her eyes sharpened on the mouse.

"Maybe just a sinister hiss. That would do." She pounced through the air, landing perfectly poised on top of her toy. Squirrelly wouldn't stand a chance.

KITTEN

O n the 6th day of life, the film over the kitten's eyes dissipated and she opened them to the world. The first thing she saw was her mother's face illuminated by a cold light filtering through the basement window. Her younger sister's lids were still closed and it could be several more days before they opened. While the older sister was given a bath, the smaller kitten mewed feebly. This bath was hurried, which was peculiar. Her mother took pride in her meticulous cleaning.

When finished she said, "Listen close, child. The humans were here in the night searching for what they called 'Christmas ornaments.' They didn't find them which means they'll be back. We must leave before we're discovered. There's a shelter not too far away. I'll take your sister first, she's weak. I'll come back for you, my love." Momma cat slid a lightweight box that jingled in front of her kitten to hide her.

"This is important—you must stay put until my return. Do not leave the cellar. Understand?"

The kitten nodded dutifully. Momma cat lifted the smaller kitten with her teeth, winked at her older daughter and padded off. The last thing Cellar Cat saw of her mom was her feathery black tail vanishing through the plastic doggie door.

A BLUSTERY DAY

It was a blustery day. Bug circled Squirrelly's home tree, calling his name. There was no response. Cellar Cat watched from her basement window seat as he placed his feet on the tree, barking for his friend. The wind silenced him. As he jumped down, his collar snagged on a prickly bush growing at the base of the tree. The more he pulled the more embedded in the prickles his collar became until he couldn't turn his neck. Cellar Cat had little interest in this scene, but as time went on and Bug began to panic, she wondered if she should get help. From where he was, he could not see her. She could take a nap and he'd be none the wiser. She did eye her warm spot on the couch but turned back. How could she sleep knowing that the foolish dog would be caught there all day?

She raced upstairs to collect the owners.

The house was empty. She ran back to the window, hoping he freed himself. No luck. In fact, he was more entangled than ever. She slowly made her way down to the doggie door and lifted the plastic. The wind blew a thick branch past her. She dropped the door. Well, that was that. She tried. The sofa was safe and inviting. She started toward it—until she heard a cry. Peeking out the door, she spied Bug hanging from the bush, exhausted. She couldn't ignore that or desert him. Cellar Cat knew what it was like to be deserted.

After the owners found her behind the jingling box of ornaments, they wrapped her in a blanket and fed her warm milk from a bottle.

The woman said to the man, "Her mother must have left to get food and either something got to her out there or she will return. We'll keep her in the cellar just in case the mom comes back."

Her fear of the unknown that may have gotten to her mother was quelled by Bug's cries. Cellar Cat had to help him.

She climbed out of the flap and slipped behind the nearest stone to protect herself from airborne objects. She tried to imagine the unknown that had taken her mother. Something large and mean with humongous razor teeth. If that thing appeared, would she hear it with all the wind? Just then came a bloodcurdling wail. Cellar Cat ducked. When it was apparent that it

was the dog's last desperate attempt to get help, she was determined to be brave. Bug needed her. She swallowed hard and dashed toward the dog, dodging flying debris as she went. Moving closer, she observed that the collar was deeply entangled. He was standing on the tips of his toes in order to breathe. She reached him and examined the collar caught in the bush. Bug looked pleased to see her but remained silent. He couldn't get enough oxygen to speak. She

24

needed to act quickly. Cellar Cat extended her longest, knife-edged nail and hacked away at the thorny bush. The thorns ripped at her skin. Each wave of her claw loosened the collar, little by little, until Bug was free and panting on the ground.

When he collected himself, he said, "You're a hero. I would have suffocated without your help. And the collar," he pulled at the Aqua blue nylon, "is one of my favorite things. You could've slashed it but you didn't. It's in perfect condition! Thanks!"

"I certainly am a hero, see my cuts? Why are you so attached to a boring ol ' collar?" She stared at the thing around his neck trying to find value in it.

"Because it means I belong. I have a family. You don't get one in the shelter. It's a privilege for pets."

Cellar Cat thought it sad to care about a boring collar.

"Look at you outside! You don't seem one bit afraid."

It was then that Cellar Cat remembered that she was indeed outdoors. The cat was witty, confident and often mean in the safety of her basement but in the big bad world, she was vulnerable.

She almost trampled Bug skittering back inside.

After much reflection, the cat decided that the fresh air, excitement and beauty of the backyard wasn't so scary after all and would often venture out. She kept a close eye on the door. Each day she progressed farther and further away until she forgot about the doggie flap and the bad thing that could be lurking outside.

BIG NEWS

One afternoon while upstairs begging for treats, Bug overheard the owners talking about news so exciting that he abandoned the treat and ran as fast as his stubby legs could muster down to the basement. He reached Cellar Cat, gasping.

"What is it? Has your little squirrel friend found an escaped convict in the attic?" she asked flatly, still weary from sleep.

"Phew," he wheezed. "You're...not...going....to believe what. just heard."

"Out with it, Bozo."

She was in no mood for theatrics.

Bug took a deep breath in, then fully exhaled. "They're—I mean we—all of us..." he swallowed hard. "We're going to visit the grand-people on the coast in two weeks!"

Bug beamed; his pink tongue hung limp between his teeth.

Cellar Cat's mouth tightened. "Wha-? You're joking."

"I'm not. Isn't it great?"

"Great?" Cellar Cat paced; her hackles raised. "Nope. No, no, this can't be happening. I can't." Her lip quivered. "We've never left home before. Why now? I don't understand. Did something happen? Why now?"

With Cellar Cat's heart practically beating out of her chest, Bug's excitement faded.

"Slow down. What's the matter? You've really never left this house?"

"I never stepped out into the backyard until recently. I went to the veterinarian once, not a fan! I had a chance to get out of the house when the front door was left open. Didn't go. I was born in this room, and I'm not leaving. I like it here and only here and I see no reason to go beyond the safety of the swans. Do you think they'll stick me in that horrendous crate? I can't! I won't!" She buried her head in her paws.

"Is your crate that bad? I like mine. It's cozy like a bear cave or a bug cave. Get it? Cause I'm Bug." Cellar Cat didn't respond. At least not in words. She didn't have to, her breathing spoke volumes.

"Think of it as an adventure. Adventures are fun, right?"

"Adventures are stupid!" Her voice was shrill. "So many bad things can happen. We could get lost, get in a car accident, 1 could get kidnapped—or worse, miss a meal! What about playtime? What about nap-time?" She clawed at the sofa. "Where will I stretch?"

"You can do all those things. I've traveled with all my different families. It's exciting. You'll see. And if anything, bad happens, we'll be together. I'll take care of you and you take care of me, like at the tree. Don't worry."

Cellar Cat pulled a stuck claw from the stretchy sofa. The image of mom's tail disappearing out the door flashed in her memory.

"'Don't worry,' he says. 'It's fun,' he says. Sure, sure, sure." She laid her chin on her protruding paws.

"You're obviously upset. Maybe I can help." Bug said. "When I was at the shelter, there were lots of scared animals. Over time, I found ways to help. I could help you too. I call it stress-aid, like a Band-Aid for your stress." He puffed out his chest proudly. "Sometimes they even work."

"Poo. Sounds hocus-pocusy." Cellar Cat pouted, then her features tightened. "Oh, I forgot about Wheezer!"

"What's a wheezer?" asked Bug.

"The grand people's little dog!" She was shouting. "And I thought you were annoying! I'll be surrounded by polar weirdos. There's no way I'm going!" Though the cat had never met Wheezer, she had observed him waiting in the grand-people's car. His body jerked in a strange fashion and he panted, most undignified.

During the next few days, whenever Bug brought up the trip or stress-aids, Cellar Cat would banish him from the basement. The closer the time came for them to leave the more distressed and irrational she became.

Odd ideas consumed her thoughts. At one point she concocted a plan to alternate hiding in dark corners throughout the basement. She reasoned if the owners couldn't find her, she wouldn't have to go. The problem was that whenever she practiced concealing herself from Bug, her glowing eyes gave her away as she was too anxious to close them.

Her next scheme was a doozy. She woke up the dog in the middle of the night.

"I'm leaving." She announced.

He stirred briefly but continued to snore. She shook him violently. Bug blinked his half-moon lids. "Huh?"

"I can't go to the grand-people's house. I'll hide in the neighborhood till you all leave, then I'll return through the doggie
door."

"You're leaving tonight?" He rubbed his forehead. "Wait, the trip isn't for a few days. What's the hurry?"

"If I run away too late, they may postpone the trip. If I'm gone long enough, they'll think I'm gone for good. They'll leave and I'll be here when they get back. There'll be a big homecoming. Everyone's happy." Her expression was a combination of desperation and hope.

"That's not a good idea," Bug said. He was awake but groggy. "It's dangerous. We don't know what's out there. What happened to you being afraid to leave the basement? You're not thinking straight. It's safer to stay together."
Cellar Cat took a step back, holding a tight stance.

"I have no choice. Besides, you said the neighborhood was safe. It's better than the car, that crate and a week away with weird Wheezer. I'll take my chances out there." Having experienced the great outdoors, it wasn't as horrible as she once imagined. She could think of worse ideas. In fact, she had just named three.

"It's not safe beyond the gate at night." He slowly got to his feet. "Think of the owners. They'll be heartbroken. You're being selfish."

He had the nerve to tell her about HER owners! The insolence of this dog to assume he knows what's best for them.

Between clenched teeth she said, "How dare you!" She pointed a sharp talon at his eye. "Selfish is taking your cat somewhere scary in a box in a moving machine."

Bug sat down. He didn't care for the menacing way she was pointing at him. "Let's take a minute to think this through and figure out a solution."

"There is. The neighborhood. If you had any brains you'd come with. Who knows what horrible fate awaits you?"

"A pleasant ride to the coast and caring grand-people await me."

He peered down as if seeing the floor for the first time, tracing an oblong stain with the pad of his foot. "Besides, I-I have to stay. Uh...I mean I can't stay. I mean I have to go. To the grand-people's house, I mean."

He fiddled with a fiber strand on the carpet. She lowered her head trying to read his face, but he avoided her gaze.

"Why?" She had no idea why he had to stay, unless he really was a bug-brained bozo.

"I'm the reason we're going. The trip is so I can meet Wheezer. It's a playdate."

Cellar Cat's body went rigid. This was about him? The owners barely knew the dog! Bug was getting an entire vacation planned around him? What was she, old news, chopped liver?

"You? This is about you?" She seethed. "I should have known. Dogs can't be trusted!" Her voice rang high and loud. "Ever since you came here, you've been nothing but a pain in my hind end. When I think of all the time, I wasted showing you patience and kindness. This is how you repay me? By being, of course, the reason for this trip. Then lying about it!"

"I don't lie. I just didn't tell you." He shivered. "I knew you'd be angry. I didn't want to add anger to all the stress you were having. That's the number one stress-aid. Don't add more stress."

"Really? That's the whole reason?"

"No." Bug backed away. "I was afraid you'd attack me."

"Of course, you were. You're pathetic. Thank God I'm leaving, I couldn't stand another minute with you!"

"I'm not pathetic!" Bug cried. "I'm a good boy. I made a mistake and I'm sorry for not telling you. I understand you're angry but—"

"But what, BOZO?"

Though tears rolled down his cheeks, a tremor of anger raced through his veins. He scowled. "Now you're being cruel. I won't tolerate cruelty. To me or anyone else!"

Bug snorted, gave a grunt then the scowl melted into a frown. He turned away, and without a second look, lumbered sadly up the stairs to the main floor.

For a nanosecond Cellar Cat thought to call out to him and apologize, but she didn't. She wished she could've told him about her mother and why she might miss her mom's return if she went to Maine. Too late. Now she was alone, scared and angry.

"The audacity of that...that...canine! I'll show him I can survive. I don't need anyone. I am smart and resourceful. I'm a cat for Pete's sake. I'm built for this."

Cellar Cat fixed her state on the doggie door. Head raised, she raced out and was swallowed up by the night.

GONE

Days passed with no sign of Cellar Cat. Her frantic owners plastered lost pet flyers all over town. The description of Cellar Cat read:

*Black and white, long-haired cat

*Moody; unreasonable

*Do not try to pet

The flyer included a pixelated picture of the cat mid-meow, eyes half-closed and nose covered in wet cat food. Underneath the photo were the owners' cell phone numbers. No one called.

Bug scoured the backyard for any sign of his friend. Though she had hurt his feelings, he sensed she was in danger and needed to be found. The only clue was a set of footprints leading out through the swan gate. Even

Squirrelly, with his connections, didn't have a trace of information about her whereabouts.

It seemed to Bug that wherever she was, she didn't want to be found. He couldn't have been more wrong.

After she left that night, Cellar Cat had spent hours wandering the foggy streets of the neighborhood. Bug was right—it wasn't as safe after dark. Shady characters walked the cobblestone streets, some hunched down in their hoodies to hide their faces. One dark figure lured her over with a promise of food only to snatch her up in a tight hug. He exhaled a sour stench onto her face, leaving her breathless in his crushing embrace. After much wiggling, she freed herself from his grip and skittered off into the unknown.

Drawn to the safety of a stairwell below a townhouse, she crouched under a step. Just as she relaxed, a woman swinging a broom chased her off, saying she'd whack the cat if she returned.

Emergency sirens woo-wooed, car alarms screeched, and red and blue lights whirled throughout the night. The sights and sounds disoriented Cellar Cat and she became hopelessly lost. Then, in the early hours, she sensed that she was being followed.

She recognized the thin slinky shadow as that of a fellow feline. It hunted her for twenty minutes through winding back alleys until she thought she might drop from exhaustion. Finally, it cornered her in a narrow passage. She had hoped to reason with the cat, but she was mistaken. It was feral and took pleasure in toying with her. Encircling Cellar Cat, it struck and stabbed her. She escaped through a broken window into a deserted church where she huddled in a muddy corner. The wild cat vanished, and though she sustained only minor

41

cuts and scratches, her pride was bruised. Scared to leave, ashamed to go home and frozen in place, she was unable to rest and worried she might never sleep again.

SURRENDERED

There were few things Bug loved more than human newborns. Maybe it was the new baby smell, the whistling sounds that came from their mouths or their peachy soft skin. Whatever the reason, he was in heaven when one was around. That's why, when he was adopted by his third family, it seemed his life took an upswing. The couple who took him in had a small baby named Anna. Jess was born soon after his adoption and a year later Nina appeared. All girls. Bug's girls. He was gentle and tolerant of their clumsy bodies and fast hands. Any human could see the love. He was such a trusted babysitter that the mother often left him in charge while she showered or stepped out of the room. He was younger and could endlessly retrieve toys, protect them from noisy mail people, and comfort them when they got hurt. Unfortunately, this utopia was to be short-lived. One-minute Bug was dragging Anna, by the collar of her shirt, away from an open window, and the next he was being dropped off at the pound by the father. No explanation, no goodbyes. Bug had been surrendered before, but this stung. He didn't like losing his girls and he would do whatever it took to not lose Cellar Cat.

HOMECOMING

Bug snuck out to search for Cellar Cat. He knew it was wrong. Only naughty dogs ran off, but the idea of losing another being in his life was unbearable. He spent the day, longer than he expected, asking passing pets in the area if they had seen her. No one had, and he returned home discouraged. To his surprise, Squirrelly was waiting for him at the swan gate. He had received a tip of a possible sighting. A homing pigeon reported a cat fitting her description entering an abandoned building several blocks away. No sooner had Squirrelly given him the coordinates to Bug that he was off. He scrambled so fast that he tripped over his own squat legs, sliding face first into the sidewalk. The fur around his mouth was covered in dirt and gravel but he didn't bother to shake it off. He kept going at a steady pace until he reached the tall and imposing church.

Inside the building, Bug brushed off any fear of danger and put nose to concrete in an attempt to sniff her out. His sense of smell hadn't worked well in years, but he wasn't ready to come to terms with that fact. It led him nowhere.

He regularly stopped to call out to her with no response. From close by, he heard a whisper. A meow so faint he wasn't sure whether he'd imagined it. But then it came again. He tried to follow the weak cry, waddling in several different directions until he caught the scent. He shuffled forward, tumbled over an old pipe, and for the second time, slid face-first into concrete. He peered up into blinking neon.

"Cellar Cat?" he asked.

"Water? Food?" she panted.

He stood up. "Come on, let's get you home."

In the light of day, Bug got a glimpse at what Cellar Cat must have gone through. Her eyes were squinty from lack of light. She was drenched head to tail in mud—some wet, some dry. The weight of the mud flattened her ears. She was covered in cuts and dried blood stained her fur. Shivering in the heat, she struggled to walk. Bug slid his solid body beside hers, allowing the cat to slump against him for support. They reached the brownstone as the sun went down, her teeth chattered in the cooler temperature.

The house was dark and silent. The owners weren't home. Cellar Cat feeble and not strong enough to make it around back. Squirrelly volunteered to squeeze through the front mail slot and unlock the door. With Bug pulling from the outside, it opened enough for the two to slip through. Once the two were safely inside,

Squirrelly edged back out, gave a bow and disappeared into the trees. Bug waved and pushed the door closed.

The weary pair made it to the kitchen. The cat's legs gave out and while on the floor, she licked the water bowl clean. She made an effort reach her food
  but was too frail. Bug, again, stood beside her, his feet planted firmly on the floor.
"I got you." he said.

She sagged against him, eating till her strength gave out. "Sleep." she said, sliding from the dog to the floor in a heap.

Bug trudged to the living room to retrieve a fuzzy green throw blanket from the couch. He lugged it back to the kitchen. Using his teeth, he encircled her within its soft layers. When he was satisfied that she was thoroughly covered, he slumped down beside her. Beneath the piles of green cotton, a shaky white paw reached out to briefly touch his before slipping back under the blanket. Bug spent the night watching over her.

At sunrise, the front door swung open. Bug heard the owner's laughs as they straggled in, arms full of shopping bags. They found him sitting stiff and serious in the front hall.

"Oh, hey buddy. Whatcha doin'?" asked the man.

When he stooped down to place a bag on the floor, Bug positioned his feet on the man's bent knees, put his muzzle to the owner's ear and yowled. He stepped down as the man stumbled backward in surprise.

"What's gotten into him?" he asked the woman while rubbing his ear.

Before she could respond, Bug stood upright on his back legs, hopped and pointed his nose toward the kitchen. The owners only shrugged their shoulders. Bug whirled a pirouette, causing him to lose his balance and fall on his back. Rolling to his feet, he simplified his tactics.

"Follow me!" he barked and ran toward the kitchen.

"I think he wants us to follow along." said the woman.

Bug led them to the sleeping cat. The reunion was a happy one, full of laughs, joy, and tears. The fun was soon interrupted by snoring. Bug, making up for several sleepless nights, dozed off under the kitchen table.

The cat and dog spent the next couple of days catching up on sleep. By the third day they were fully rested.

Cellar Cat was her surly self, but Bug, usually keen to spend time with her, spent the better part of his day upstairs or in the garden. When in the basement with the cat, he was polite but absent of his usual warmth.

It wasn't hard for Cellar Cat to guess why. He hadn't forgiven her for the insults she spewed at him many nights ago. This miffed her. He was just a simple-minded, petty mutt and his holding a grudge proved it. He wasn't sophisticated enough to forgive and forget. Besides, who did he think he was coming to get her? She was capable of taking care of herself and Bug knew it. She never asked to be rescued. He wanted to play the hero, that's all. Well, if he expected her to thank him for that, he was sadly mistaken.

Still, below the tough exterior, a part of her wondered if she had something to apologize for. Did she go too far? She wasn't sure. Was he playing the hero or did he, perhaps, care for her? She didn't know if she could trust these wonderings. They made her feel vulnerable, and she wasn't used to it.

THE CRATE

The day of the trip brought a flurry of activity. During coffee, the owners planned their driving route. In the early morning, they rushed around marking off checklists, packing suitcases and loading the car.

Bug hummed to himself as he gathered his few possessions. He set aside special toys to bring: a rubber ball, his favorite half-gnawed bone and a spotless pocket-sized white stuffed bunny given to him on his adoption day.

He placed and replaced the items in his crate. Cellar Cat, towering over him in an armchair, followed his movements with disdain as he repeatedly reorganized his belongings. When at last satisfied with the arrangement, he went beneath the stairs, found the hamper, and pulled the unwashed, mud-stained green blanket that he used to wrap Cellar Cat in days before. He dragged it into the crate with him and settled in. He nuzzled it while eagerly awaiting the owners.

"I'm not going, you know." Cellar Cat said matter-of-factly.

"Suit yourself." He hugged the blanket closer. "I will fight this every step of the way. Mark my words, they won't get me into that crate!"

"You do what you have to." he said stiffly. "Just don't harm the owners."

"Humph."

She was sick of his forced politeness and tried to imagine his great disappointment if the trip were canceled.

"Ready to go?" the man asked Bug. He closed the crate door. Cellar Cat felt her belly flutter and her eyes went to the last place she saw her mother.

The owner unlocked the wheels and rolled the crate out. The cat jumped to the window, giving her a full view of the backyard. She watched as Bug wagged his tail wildly all the way to the car. His excitement felt like betrayal. She raged.

The man reappeared. He grabbed her crate. "Your turn, girl."

Want to make a bet? she mused.

There was a five-minute standoff where both pair stared each other down. When the man dove to grab her, the situation escalated. Cellar Cat dodged his outreached hand, howling, hissing, and striking at him with her claws. Taken aback, the owner briefly retreated upstairs, returning with a sheet and wearing leather gloves. He threw the sheet over her and gathered her up like a package. The cat moaned while he held her over the crate. He lowered her carefully toward the open door. With all legs flailing, she managed to free herself from the sheet but the owner still had a grip on the scruff of her neck. Attempting to bite the hand that held her, she swung her body up and down and back and forth, eventually clawing his arm. Blood spilled from the wound. The owner dropped her. She tumbled toward the crate in slow motion, slamming her head then her hip on the hard plastic before landing softly on the carpet. She lay motionless.

There was a black, heavy silence. A soft clicking. Click-click-click. Cellar Cat opened one eyelid then closed it. The light was blinding. More clicks. What was it? She had to know. Cautiously, she flickered her lashes open to hazy, bright movements. There was another sound. A garbled voice. Wherever it was coming from, it was speaking to her. A blurry outline took shape. A human face. Words formed in its mouth.

"C'mon, kitty." It was a woman's voice. She wore a blazing white lab coat made brighter by the fluorescent lighting. The clicking came from her pen. Cellar Cat recognized the woman. It was Dr. Lee, her veterinarian.

"You had a tumble but you're going to be fine". Dr. Lee said.

Cellar Cat didn't feel fine. Her head was pounding and there was a sharp pain in her hip.

"Can we take her home?" It was the owner's voice but she couldn't see him. He sounded anxious.

"We are supposed to be going to Maine today." It was the woman.

"Sorry, but I'd like to keep her overnight for observation." said the veterinarian. "With rest and medication, she'll recover fully. No worries. By tomorrow, she'll be as good as new."

The cat should've been celebrating her victory. She'd not be going to Maine today, but in her pain-induced stupor she felt only defeat.

Dr. Lee gave Cellar Cat an injection, which she braced for but never felt. The owners each gave her a kiss on the cheek as she was carried out of the exam room and into a cavernous room in the back of the animal hospital where sick and injured pets were kept. She was placed in a top cage. There was a litter pan, a metal bowl, and a folded towel. Cellar Cat placed a paw on the sleeve of Dr. Lee's lab coat, digging into the stiff fabric, being careful not to hurt the woman. The veterinarian expertly removed her paw, one toe at a time.

"You'll be fine, I promise. Get some sleep." Dr. Lee blessed her with a few light pets, closed the cage door, and disappeared into her office.

The cat took in her surroundings. The bottom cells were occupied by dogs of all sizes while cats populated the upper cages. Each animal was in a state of distress or discomfort. Some barked, others meowed. A few simply whimpered. Cellar Cat did none of those. She sulked. Strange emotions boiled up inside her. Though her mind was dull from the medication, it was full of questions. Would she walk again? When would she go home? What would happen if her mom returned to the basement to find Cellar Cat not there? Who should she blame?

The last question was the easiest to answer. It was the owner's fault. He should've been more careful. If he didn't feed her, she'd be done with him all together. Still, he must be feeling pretty guilty right about now—unlike that traitor, Bug. What did he think about all this? Was he mad, sad, both? Surely the trip was canceled and she was certain he wasn't acting so smug and superior at that moment. Served him right too! She tried to envision him moping in his now worthless crate. Strange as it was, she had a hard time feeling good about Bug feeling bad. In fact, visualizing his pain made her tummy hurt. She had never felt this way before and didn't understand it. Remembering the relief, she felt when Bug found her in the church, guided her home and nursed her made the night at the hospital a little better.

FORGIVENESS

The realization that Bug could be annoying and slow but also faithful, reliable and patient created a shift in Cellar Cat's brain. She couldn't explain it to herself, but she saw the dog in a different light. She saw herself differently too. Those rude things she'd said to him. Would he ever forgive her? She wished he were here now. She wished she had gotten in the crate. A few short hours ago, she would have done anything to stay home and wait for her mother like she always had. Now she wondered if her mom was ever coming back? Should she wait in the basement forever? Would it be so horrible to go to Maine? If her mom came back, she'd see Cellar Cat's toys and know she lived there. All wouldn't be lost.

The cheerless cage, in a room that smelled of urine and bleach, made the cat miss the safety of the basement and her cozy sofa. The flicker of tube lighting cast long shadows. A chinchilla's continuous squeaking and teeth grinding set her on edge, as did a ragged mutt's licking and chewing. Across from her, a bony cat with a tube from its forearm to a hanging bag watched her with lifeless eyes. Twice in the night a ghostly bird cackled, "Bad Kitty! Bad Kitty!"

Cellar Cat yawned. The medication took effect and she slipped into a dreamless sleep. Dr. Lee checked on her throughout the evening, and at dawn gave the cat one last injection. When she woke again, the pain was gone.

Misty morning sun beat down on the owner's gray Cadillac. The man opened the hatchback.

"Here we go." He said, placing Cellar Cat's crate gingerly next to Bug's.

She had meowed non-stop from the hospital's back room to the car. She no longer cared where they were going as long as it was far away from that horrible place. Never again would she fight getting into a crate.

"Nice and easy girl." The man peeked through the holes of the crate. "Hope you aren't upset with me."

"Meow."

He smiled as if he understood. Cellar Cat hoped he did. She was saying that it was her fault. Now she had to tell Bug the same thing.

Before she could say a word, Bug spoke. "I'm glad you're ok."

She peered from her crate into his. There were dark circles under his eyes.

"I'm fine." she said quietly, touching her hip. "Uh, Bug, I-I'm..." She gulped. "Maybe I shouldn't have called you names."

There were many more things she wanted to say, like "I appreciate all that you did for me." "I've missed you" or "Thank you," but all she could muster was a measly "I'm sorry."

"Yay!" he yipped merrily. His response surprised the cat. The dark bags were gone. He looked younger, stronger.

"I know this trip and me coming into your life has been hard on you." The warmth in his voice had returned. "Your life changed, which can be difficult, but you learned something and changed with it. That's not easy."

It was true. She felt different. Lighter, softer, more peaceful. It was also true that it wasn't easy to get there, but somehow, she did with Bug's help.

"You've grown. I'm happy for you and—" He placed a paw on his crate towards her. "—proud."

Turning away, she sighed and said, "No need to go overboard. Geesh! But there is one thing I'd like."

"What's that?"

"Let's try to get along. Is that ok?"

"Of course!"

Delighted, Bug hopped up and down with so much force that the man asked, "What's going on back there?"

Bug replied with a spirited bark.

"You know, maybe I could use your stress-aids after all." Cellar Cat said. "But don't go making a big deal about it."

"Sure." Bug said assuredly though his body trembled with enthusiasm. Laying flat on his blanket, he clasped his paws together.
"Let's start with a grounding exercise. Place your paws firmly on the ground, spreading out your feet. Breathe."

His measured voice, which she used to find unpleasant, was now soothing. "Think of your toes as growing roots into the earth. Breathe." He closed his eyes. "The plan is to eventually name your fears, talk to them, and break them down bit by bit. Baby steps—always baby steps. We've got the entire ride, so take your time and don't forget to breathe."
Cellar Cat did as instruct, but in truth, she didn't need the strategies. Just being with him and

65

knowing they were friends again was enough to
calm her all the way to Maine.

MAINE

With Bug's help, the car ride was more manageable than Cellar Cat had imagined. She snoozed a good deal of the way, waking as they arrived in town.

"Wow, that ocean is beautiful. "said the man.

Bound in their crates, Bug and Cellar Cat could only hear the sea wind and smell the salty air through the open windows.

"Just look at those darling fishing boats." the woman said.

Even when craning their necks, only the boat masts were visible to the animals.

The car turned onto a winding gravel driveway and the owner parked under a gnarled apple tree.

They had arrived. When the trunk opened, Bug and Cellar Cat faced a white clapboard farmhouse surrounded by the green grass of an expansive pasture. In the corner of one field stood a modest red barn enclosed by a fence. Rows of fruit trees waved at a never-ending wilderness. Cellar Cat swished her tail.

It was new and strange. She didn't like new and strange.

The grand-people hobbled from the house to greet them. They were older and more shriveled than she remembered but just as spunky. At their feet was a small fawn-colored dog twitching from ear to tail. The dog's bulgy, saucer eyeballs were fixed in their direction.

"Wheezer." she whispered; her lips curled in a sneer.

"He seems nice." Bug said. "Give him a chance. You might like him."

"Really? He's never not strange." Cellar Cat was reminded of the time before Bug when she believed all dogs weren't to be trusted. But having faith in him did not mean she had to trust other dogs. Wheezer was still on her bad list.

The man opened Bug's crate, lifted him out and set him on the gravel. Bug stretched then playfully zigzagged around the grand- people's feet, lapping up all the attention they paid him. He paused in front of Wheezer. Though it was mid-summer and sticky hot, the dog trembled.

"H-h-how do you do?" said Wheezer.

"Stiff but glad to be here." Bug's whole body wagged with joy.

After greeting the owners with hugs and kisses, the grand-lady limped over to the cat's crate.

"Hello, kitty, it's been a while." The old woman peeped in, her curly locks hung into the crate in long silvery strands. Cellar Cat batted at the hair. The grand-lady laughed out loud. "Still a naughty girl, I see. Let's get you out of there. You've had a long journey." Waving away the owners' protests, the grand-lady opened the crate. "She'll be fine."

Cellar Cat slunk down to the springy grass and froze. So much was unfamiliar. The fresh and briny air, the tinkle of wind chimes, the aromatic scent of pine and wide-open fields. Feeling overwhelmed, she scuttled over to hide behind the owners.

"Maybe we should bring her in the house, Mom." Said the woman.

"Nonsense. The porch is set up for them. The screen door is left ajar and they can come and go as they please. You worry too much."

"I just think—" the owner began.

"No. I'm sorry dear, but this is what becomes of a kitten left by its mother too early. She's a scaredy-cat and needs to toughen up. Poor thing." The old woman's cheeks sagged. "But this new dog of yours is special." She grinned at Bug. "He'll straighten her out."

From the front door, the grand-man motioned for the owners to follow him into the house. They did so with pickled faces, leaving Cellar Cat, Bug, and Wheezer on their own.

"Meow!" Cellar Cat called after them. She yearned for safety.

Bug spoke calmly. "Grand-lady said not to worry. Remember your stress strategies. Feel your emotions. They will pass. Focus on your breathing. Baby steps."

She did as he said, giving herself time to breathe. When she was ready, she nodded and Wheezer eagerly led the way.

Hanging ferns and blue-moon wisteria greeted them outside the screened-in porch. Inside was a cheerful pet hideaway with a choice of dog beds, blankets, and toys. There was a new cat tree complete with a hammock that, according to Wheezer, was purchased especially for Cellar Cat. She found its high platforms intimidating, preferring a small donut dog bed instead.

From the door, the sprawling backyard lay before them. Strewn about the lawn were muddy, torn and forgotten toys. Though the three pets were excited to play, it had been a long trip and it was getting late, so they agreed to turn in early. Exploring could wait till morning.

SEA CAT

They woke early. Cellar Cat snuggled up in bed, studied white-throated sparrows fluttering from tree to tree. Wheezer, much to Bug's delight, flaunted his collection of playthings.

He nosed a shiny rubber ball. "This is new. And the nylon bone," He hurled it back into his toy pile. "is a reward for sitting for three minutes straight."

"Oh, nice," said Bug. "You are very—" He started but noticed a shock of yellow beneath a pile of shabby playthings. "What's that?" He asked, pointing to it.

Wheezer didn't answer but went about pulling the large toy from its hiding place. It was a life-sized stuffed orange tabby cat wearing a cable-knit sweater, a bright yellow slicker, bib, and hat.

The clothing was like new but the stuffed cat had much of its stuffing chewed out.

"I-it's my sea cat." He said.

"A sea cat?" asked Bug.
Cellar Cat, listening from her bed, turned and studied the tattered cat with suspicion. She had been right not to trust him.
Bug looked from the stuffed toy to Cellar Cat and snicked..

"What's so funny?" she asked.

"I don't know, but I think this outfit would fit you." He sized up the toy. "Yup, you should try it on."

"Nope!"

"Well, I'm not surprised. She's afraid of everything." Wheezer said. "At least that's what my owners say."

"Am not! Clothes are stupid. Cats don't wear clothes." She gnashed her teeth at the dogs. "Only dumb humans and dogs wear them."

"True. Cats don't wear clothes, but that's why it'd be funny." said Bug.

"S-s-scaredy cat." Wheezer teased.

"Am not!"

"Prove it." he said.

Both dogs sat motionless awaiting her response. In truth, she was afraid to be seen in clothing. It was unbecoming of a cat —any cat, and not just dignified ones like herself. If she backed down,

Wheezer would torture her the whole week, calling her names, and making fun of her. Bug would never make fun of anyone but what would he think of her? Perhaps this was a way of making up for the way she'd treated him back home.

"Fine." She gestured at the stuffed cat. "Give me the darn things."

Wheezer stripped the toy, handing the clothing to Cellar Cat one at a time. She slipped them on with surprising ease, as if they'd been sewn for her.

"Well?" She spun in a circle. The sweater was itchy and with every movement, the raincoat's plastic rubbed against itself, making a horrible scrunching sound. The hat hung low over her forehead. "It looks ridiculous, doesn't it?"

Bug suppressed a chuckle. Wheezer chortled out loud.

"Ok, I'm taking it off." She threw the hat.

Suddenly, a loud bellow came booming out of the barn. It gave Bug and Cellar Cat a start. Neither had ever heard anything like it.

"What was that?" Bug asked.

Wheezer said, "Oh, that's just—"

The little dog never finished his sentence because Bug, without needing further explanation, burst through the dog door onto the springy grass and ran at turbo turtle speed toward the barn. Wheezer was fast at his heels. Cellar Cat followed. Due to the plastic outfit limiting her mobility, she had a hard time keeping up.

Inside, the barn was filled from floor to rafters with hay. Bales of alfalfa flowed down from the hayloft, and round bundles of straw were stacked all along edges. Several inches of the dry spongy grass packed the floor.

77

The sole occupant, a brown butter-colored cow, chewed its cud at the far end of the barn. It let out a low moo. It was noise they had heard on the porch.

"Is it dangerous?" asked Cellar Cat. "Does it bite?"

"No. That's a cow."

The sheer size of the animal alarmed the cat, and as the dogs walked closer, she lagged behind.

Wheezer stopped in the middle of the barn.

"We shouldn't get any closer. She's liable to kick."

"I heard that cows were gentle." Bug said.

"She doesn't mean anything by it. Small animals make her nervous."

"Who this be then?" came a salty voice from behind a hay bale.

"Who's asking?" said Cellar Cat.

"It's Bumbles." whispered Wheezer. "Careful."

Out from around the bale sauntered a heavily matted cat. His long dull gray coat was teeming with dandruff and fleas. A raised pink scar snaked its way from one closed eyelid to the corner of his down-turned bottom lip. He had a crooked tail and was missing a chunk out of his right ear.

"I'm askin', that be who." he said gruffly. "And I say again, who ye be, lass?" Before she could respond, Wheezer took off like a shot into the nearest hay pile.

"That there be a cowardly dog." Bumbles said before turning to the visitors. "Now state ye business in me barn."

"Your barn?" Cellar Cat turned to the cow, but it continued to munch its hay unperturbed.

"I be askin' the questions round here. What ye be doing in me barn? I gotta hunch ye be hornswoggling me mice. I don't much like bilge-suckers or scurvy dogs." He bore into Bug with his one good eye, unblinking as a flea skittered across it. Bug trembled.

"The-They're not hunting, Bumbles. They're the invited guests of my owners." Wheezer mumbled from the hay pile.

"Is that so?" Bumbles puffed out his chest. "They're not me owners, and I answer to no man, ye understand?" It was at that moment that

Bumbles noticed Cellar Cat's outfit. He scowled at her.

"Sink me! Whatcha wearing, lass? 'Cause that be sea cat's garb, and ye ain't no sea cat."

Her skin baked under the plastic. "Maybe I am." Her paws were thick with sweat. "I'm not. But how would you know?"

"'Cause I was once a sea cat meself. Catchin' fish and keepin' me owner's boat free of vermin. That's how I know." With one frayed nail, he straightened out his whiskers. "Aye, a darn good old salt I were too. Me owner be proud tah have me."

Wheezer snuck out from his hiding spot and whispered to Bug.

"Good for you." Cellar Cat said.

"And I can tell ye ain't one. Just a landlubber in sea cat's clothing."

"I'm not a landlover, or whatever you called me."

She searched her mind for something mean and biting to say. "You talk nonsense and smell bad!" was what came out. "Who would want to be a dumb sea cat anyway?"

Bumble's face turned from disgust to red rage. Her comments hit a nerve. She knew she went too far and felt a pang of remorse.

"It be noble work and a right nasty job. Wranglin' rats, haulin' fish. It be only for a true brave heart. Not for the likes of ye."

"I could if I wanted to. I can do anything." Her nose twitched. "I just don't want to."

"Aye, so you be a scaredy-cat, aye?"

"Am not! Why does everyone call me that?"

"If the peg leg fits, wear it." he replied.

"What does that even mean?"
"If-n ye be a coward, that's what ye be."

"No clearer, thanks. I'm probably braver than you." She held her nose high. "By a lot."

Bug could see that Cellar Cat was getting worked up. Knowing it wouldn't end well, he opened his mouth to interject, but she put up a paw to silence him.
"That so? I doubt it." the barn cat said.

"Too bad there's no way to prove it. Well, we should get going." Cellar Cat waved Bug and Wheezer toward the house.

"Ah, but there be." Bumbles cocked an eye. "At the end of that their driveway, past that there street, and down a wee hill, be a fishin' trawler."

"So?"

"That trawler be leavin' at high noon and returnin' at dusk. If ye think ye got what it takes to be a sea cat, ye be on it."

Three sets of eyes bore into Cellar Cat: one daring her to go, one imploring her to stay, and the other chewing a blade of hay as if he were eating popcorn in a cinema.

"I-I—"

An image of her snuggled up in the cushy donut bed popped into her head. How did she get into these messes? Why couldn't she be resting?

Now was the time for Bug to interfere. If he could put on a show and demand that she stays, she could give in and come out of this without looking like a wimp. She willed him to interject but without understanding the silent plea,he shrugged his shoulders.

"If-n one o' yer friends would rather take the chicken's place. Aight one of ya brave 'nuff?" Wheezer turned and galloped toward the farmhouse, tail tucked between his legs.

Bug took a step. *He better not volunteers.* She thought. *He's too clumsy; too old.* When he opened his mouth to speak, Cellar cat stepped in.

"Ok."she said. "I'm not scared. I'll catch more fish and kill more rats than you ever dreamed of, buster. You'll see."

"That be foolhardy ta believe. But ye be back tonight, alive and holdin' a fish and yo-ho-ho, I be struck dumb." He scanned the horizon. "Ye better get moving, lass. It be coming on noon." Cellar Cat looked up to the sky, turned to sneer at Bumbles, then ran toward the ship's masts in the distance.

"Wait!" Bug called. She could've ignored him but she didn't want to walk alone.

She slowed. He reached her, chest heaving.

"Are you really going on that boat? Remember what happened last time you didn't think things through?"

"Poo. This is different." she said.

"How?" asked Bug.

"Did you hear what that son of a hamster wheel called me?"

"He isn't very nice, but don't let anger keep you from thinking clearly."

Cellar Cat walked on without responding. Bug trailed her. The rocky driveway turned onto a sand road. They sprinted across it to a hill above the waterfront, where three docked boats floated below, including the fishing trawler.

Cellar Cat, struggling to maneuver in the sea clothing, reached the hill after Bug. He peeked over the ridge and said, "Blech, I don't like heights." He backtracked to where Cellar Cat was, putting his body between her and the hill. "Listen."

She had no intention of listening until she got a peek at the rocking docks below. She sat. The dock could wait.

"You have a minute." she said.

"Thanks."

A truck pulled into a dusty parking lot along the shore. Fishing rods and gear filled the truck. Cellar Cat chewed her lip.

"But talk fast. That looks like the fisherman."

"How to start." He tapped his temple. "Ok, got it. When I was at my first shelter, I had a mentor."
"A what?"

"A mentor. Someone who provides guidance. You know, a role model."

"Could have just said that. Talk faster."

"Anyhoo, my mentor was a Dalmatian named Daisy. She knew for days that she was headed for the 'room.'"

"What?"

A young man and an older gentleman unloaded coolers and bags from the truck bed.

"I forgot you don't know about shelters. Every shelter has a room—a room that you go in but don't come out of."

"Well, that got dark fast. Go on."

"I've had a few close calls with that door myself."

"Sorry." Perspiration dripped from her nose.

"Thanks. She was lovely. Daisy, I mean. I learned—"

Cellar Cat stood up. She didn't want to go but time was ticking away. Why did the dog think as slow as he ran? Bug shook his head, understanding that he needed to speed up.

"Before she left for the room, Daisy became real peaceful. She told me that she regretted spending her life worrying about what others thought of her. She said to me, 'Don't live your life for others. Let them worry about themselves.' That's good advice for you. It's not your job to change Bumble's mind. He's got a right to think of you any way he wants, even if he doesn't like you."

Cellar Cat crossed her forepaws. She felt she was being preached to.

Bug saw her shut down and spoke faster.

"The other shelter dogs didn't like me. I can be—" He took a breath. "—annoying. That's why I considered their criticism in case I needed to change a certain behavior. Daisy taught me to focus on the work I needed to do for myself, not for them."

"Stop nagging me. The boat is leaving."

"Ok." Bug didn't move.

"One more thing. Wheezer told me that Bumbles worked hard on a boat his whole life. When the owner retired, he dumped Bumbles off at the farm. No sorry, goodbye or thank you. Just opened the car door and shoved him out. He hasn't left that barn since. He's hurt and angry and wants to hurt others because of it."

Cellar Cat thought of her mother leaving, never to return. "He wants you to feel the pain he feels. If you go on that boat, no matter what happens, he wins. I want you to win." Her memory faded. To Cellar Cat, it seemed Bug didn't appreciate the fact that she volunteered for this to save him from doing it himself. It didn't occur to her that his intention back at the barn wasn't to volunteer but to argue for the two cats to stop their nonsense.

"No faith in me, huh? Well, I don't care. No one calls me names."

She pushed past Bug, bumping his shoulder. He winced."Be careful."

Cellar Cat was hurt. She hoped he'd think she was brave for once. It sure would make it easier to get on that boat if he did.

"I'll be fine. I'm a cat. I'm built for this. You wouldn't understand. You're just a dog."

A few steps from the crest of the hill, a nervous Bug watched Cellar Cat sneak down to the shore. She hesitated at the dock. It was wobbly and unsteady. She tested the buoyancy with a foot. The dock moved with the tide. If it weren't for the humiliation, she would have turned back. But with her reputation at stake, she pressed on. Her steps were slow and purposeful, as if she were walking a tightrope. The fishermen, dressed in green bibs, were on board securing traps and untangling nets. Cellar Cat stepped as close as she could get to the trawler. She reached up, ready to jump aboard. The engine roared to life. She nearly fell in the water from shock. She collected herself, and with only seconds to spare, clawed her way up a wooden post and hopped on board. Luckily, men had their backs to the cat. The boat thrust forward, sending her tumbling behind a tower of lobster traps. A hard landing but a perfect hiding place.

One fisherman disappeared into the helm while the other untied ropes securing the boat to the dock. After a few jolts, they chugged away from the shore heading for open waters. It was while cowering behind the rancid smelling traps, that Cellar Cat decided she'd made a mistake. She watched the coastline gradually disappear. Bug, on the hill, got smaller and smaller. Her eyes locked on him until he was no more than a speck on the horizon.

The farther out they went, the bumpier the waves became. The cat teetered, woozy from the rolling water. From her spot she caught movement in her periphery. A long pink tail snaked its way down into the hull. A rat. A filthy rat. It was her chance to prove she had what it took to be a sea cat but at that moment she was in no shape to chase after it. Since the safest place for her was hunkered down behind the traps, she told herself that she would only venture out for fish. That was all Bumbles required.

After what seemed like hours but was much less, the boat slowed, jerking several times. The contents of Cellar Cat's belly lurched in unison with the boat. The men threw a net overboard, and a short time later pulled it back in. A scant number of large fish that floundered at the bottom of the mesh were emptied onto the deck. One slid over to her. She lunged for it but it glided past her. She watched crossed- eyed as it flopped over the boat's edge back into the sea.

The trawler rocked forward, cruised, then idled a second time. The net was thrown and pulled up again. It was a larger haul but with smaller fish. Feeling brave, the cat poked her head around. She tried to grasp a fish that had flapped close to her, touching it with her paw. It was slick and slimy. She withdrew. It flipped backwards, right into the fisherman's hands and was then thrown into a waiting cooler. Disoriented, the cat withdrew again.

The process was repeated once more. The catch was greater, the fish were smaller, a perfect size for a cat to claw. She creeped out again, successfully spearing a fish with her nail.

95

Unfortunately, the deck had become slippery with water and fish oil. She held a trap for support, accidentally pulling it out from under the tower of traps. Like a house of cards, the tower collapsed and she slid out into the deck, in full view of the men. Cellar Cat retreated, but it was too late. She was caught.

A rugged fisherman with a windburned face peered around the corner. The fish Cellar Cat had hooked was still attached to her and flailed about, taking her arm with it. The man smirked. He crouched down, removed the fish and offered it to her. The second the slimy thing touched her mouth, she spit it out. She ran to the side of the boat, taking giant gulps of salty air. Succumbing to sea sickness, she slumped to the deck, runny nosed and drooling.

Ocean water had long since seeped through the plastic slicker, soaking her fur. She shivered. The man picked her up and brought her into the boat's interior. He lay her on a cushioned bench and covered her with a thick woolen sweater. He pointed out the window.

"Lay here apiece, crittah. Be a wicked good idea to watch the horizon." he said before climbing back up on deck.

Though she watched the horizon with great intensity, it was some time before she felt better. Once the nausea dissipated, she removed the heavy sea cat clothing. She deposited them in a wastebasket and crawled back under the wool sweater. She lay there shivering till the sun went down.

The voyage back gave her time to reflect on how she had gotten there. It had been her fault again but hadn't Bumbles egged her on? No one stopped him.

A voice interrupted her thoughts. It nagged at her. It told her that if she took the time to think things through, she wouldn't be in this mess. Was she really to blame? And why did this voice sound like Bug? One thing was for sure, she shouldn't have listened to Bumbles.

The boat returned to the dock that evening. Cellar Cat had warmed up considerably. Her fur had fully dried, though the static from the wool turned her into a black and white puffball. The nice fisherman came to collect her. He placed her on the dock and again offered her a fish. The cat sneered. The sight of it made her gag. As a thank you for his kindness, she allowed him one pet to which they both received an unpleasant electric shock.

Bug, waiting from shore, waved wildly and didn't stop until she stumbled to him. Her legs jiggled.

The dog wagged his tail.

"How was it?"

She didn't answer, choosing instead to swallow her queasiness.

"You'll get your land legs back shortly. Go slow."
"Couldn't go fast if I wanted to."
She guzzled big mouthfuls of fresh air, then retched.

"Are you ok?"

"Do I look ok?" Her eyes were crossed and her nose was running.
"You look alive." he replied.

His words slurred in her ears. Everything seemed swirly. All she wanted to do was lie down. For the second time in a week Bug let her lean on him as he guided her toward the farm.

"No fish?"

"Nope." So what? Bumbles didn't care about her. Wheezer didn't either. Bug was here and he didn't care about the boring old fish. At the farmstead, her focus sharpened. Her belly was still tight.

"What about Bumbles? He'll have something to say about it." Bug said.

"You know what?" She burped. "I've come to realize that I can't waste my time worrying about what one bonehead thinks of me. I've got my own problems."

"You figured that out? All by yourself?"

"Yup. I don't care about that big dope anymore. I care about a nice soft donut bed."

The porch was a welcome sight, and once absorbed into the round bed, she let out a few more loud belches then fell into a long deep slumber.

But before she closed her eyes she said to Bug, "I learned my lesson. From now on it's all about me. No one else matters."
He grimaced. "Uh, that's not what I—"
"Joking. J-o-k-i-n-g."
"Good night, Cellar."

"Night, night Bug." she said dreamily. He grinned.

A BULLY

Eager to meet the day, Bug, Cellar Cat and Wheezer woke early. They sat in awe as the farm came to life. Mist, hovering above the fields dissipated in the sun. Birds darted from tree to earth in search of food, dew drops evaporated in the rising heat and a lone rooster crowed in the distance.

After a quick breakfast, the trio ran to the backyard. The boys played tug of war with a stick while Cellar Cat stalked a black bird by the barn.

Bumbles stuck his head out from behind the barn door and called out, "Aye, what the scaredy-cat be doing now? Chasin' birdies, is she?"

Though the words stung, she ignored him and the feeling passed. She decided to hunt behind the barn, out of his sight.

Pursuing the bird quieted her mind. She stalked him through the back field to a high wooden fence that bordered a neighboring yard. He fluttered to the top of the fence, squawked, flew straight upward then swooped down, missing the crown of her head by inches. She scurried to the side of the fence, crouching against it for protection. Her heart was beating fast. The bird flew up to repeat his dive- bomb but just as he was to descend, he caught sight of something on the other side of the fence and flew away.

Cellar Cat, still in a low position, arched her neck to examine the fence. There were three teeny holes drilled into the lowest part. Two openings close together—one below. She moved to investigate but was interrupted by frenzied barking. She turned to see Wheezer jumping up and down pointing to the fence with one foot and beckoning her back with another. She wheeled around, in the holes, were two eyes and a nose. Her mouth went dry. She couldn't make out what it was that was glowering at her but she wasn't going to stick around to find out. She made for the boys at the far end of the yard. Turning as she went; she saw a small brown blur rapidly gaining on her. She skidded to a halt beside Bug. Lowering her head, she hissed just as the blur stopped and took shape.

A long-haired teacup chihuahua with ears, twice the size of its apple-shaped head, growled at them. It opened mouth revealed a row of itty-bitty razor-sharp teeth. It was a terrifying if not adorable abomination that was fixated not on Cellar Cat but on Bug. Large doe eyes bore into him.

"What'd I do?" Bug asked, bewildered.

"I don't like the looks of you." it lisped. "You're ugly."

Bug's cheeks flushed. "My looks?"

Wheezer leaned in, speaking quietly. "That's E-emmy. My neighbor. She's a b- bully."

Emmy's tiny body was stiff and alert. The chihuahua's soft cocoa hair blew in the wind. Her chocolate-chip nose whistled intimidatingly. Wheezer whimpered. "D-don't make eye contact."

Unfortunately, Bug's knee-jerk reaction was to do exactly that. The dog's eyes flashed up, momentarily meeting Emmy's. His lids widened; hers narrowed. He immediately averted his gaze but the damage was done. She lunged for his muzzle. He sprung up, lost his balance and flopped onto his back. There Bug lay, stunned, paws twitching like an overturned beetle. Cellar Cat helped him roll onto his feet. "Ha-ha, stupid." Emmy said.

Cellar Cat, feeling protective over her friend, put her body between Bug and the small dog. But the chihuahua was fast and lunged again. This time aiming for Bug's cheek, she missed. Bug spun around and headed for the porch. He rushed through the doggie door, climbing clumsily beneath a pile of toys. Cellar Cat and Wheezer weren't far behind.

Emmy stood her ground, straight and proud. A pocket-sized nightmare.

"Next time I thee you, my bite won't miss!" She stomped back to the fence and before disappearing beneath it said, "I'll be waiting." Seconds later her eyes and nose reappeared in the holes. She stuck out her tongue, then as quickly as she appeared, she was gone.

"Wow. What was that?" Cellar Cat's bewilderment was mirrored in Wheezer's face. Bug, still hidden behind the toys, whimpered.

"Usually, it's me she's after." Wheezer said.

"How does she get away with it?" Cellar Cat asked.

"Cause she's cute."

"Yeah, I'll give her that." said Cellar Cat. "Literally, adorable. But nasty. I pity Bug. She's coming for him, hardcore."

Bug stepped out from the toys; his nose drippy.

"It's not funny. I thought she was going to kill me. She went for my jugular."

"She didn't come close." Cellar Cat snickered. "If she wanted to, she would've landed the bite." Realizing her words didn't reassure her friend, she pushed a rubber ball in his direction. "Don't worry, I'm sure she's moved on to tormenting another dog. Maybe one her own size."

Bug picked up the ball and went to mope on his bed.

"Thankfully, she only comes once a year. Wait, that must mean it's the Fourth of July. My owners will be going to a picnic tonight." Said Wheezer.

They agreed, for safety's sake, to stay on the porch for the remainder of the morning. As noon approached, Wheezer surprised Cellar Cat by volunteering to venture out. She couldn't help but wonder if he had been embarrassed by his previous behavior and was trying to prove his bravery. He inched his way to mid-yard. Thinking the coast was clear, he gave a thumbs-up. Suddenly, as if out of a horror flick, two eyes and a nose reappeared in the fence. In a blink, Wheezer was back on the porch. Emmy never even had to leave her side of the fence.

By late afternoon, the group was restless and bored. They needed to get off the porch and do something.

Wheezer said. "N-now might be a good time. It's about her napping hour."

The cat and two dogs crept along, Bug taking up the rear. Cellar Cat and Wheezer tip-toed to midpoint and waited. When there was no sign of the chihuahua or her fence face, they motioned for Bug to hurry along while cheering noiselessly.

The afternoon was theirs and they resolved to enjoy every bit of freedom. The trio vowed to check the fence every so often. They played dodgeball, tag, follow the leader, leapfrog, and huckle buckle beanstalk with gusto. In time they forgot all about Emmy.

Never having played with other animals, Cellar Cat had to be constantly coaxed by Bug to share, play fair and to practice good sportsmanship. Wheezer, being an only dog, had to be reminded too. It was while being the seeker during hide-and-seek that the cat spotted a wagon leaning against a maple tree. It gave her an idea. She cornered Wheezer and murmured in his ear. He smiled, nodded, ran to the barn and returned with a small halter and lead rope.

"This was the cow's when she was a calf." He secured the rope to the wagon.

"What's it for?" asked Bug.

"P-put it on. You're going to pull us." Wheezer held out the halter.

"Oh, no thank you." Bug waved the other dog away.

"We're going to play king of the wagon! Right, Wheez, old pal?" Cellar Cat's face was illuminated by mischief. "You'll be the horse, of course." Bug shook his head furiously. He felt uneasy that they were suddenly in cahoots and ganging up on him.

"Come on. You're the only one big enough to pull it."

Bug pursed lips and crossed his arms.

"So, it was fine for me to put on those dumb sea cat clothes and humiliate myself for you? I guess you're too good to do something not nearly as embarrassing to help your friends."
"Yeah, how about it?" Wheezer chimed in.
Bug uncrossed his arms. "I guess, but— "
"No buts! We're doing this." The cat stepped to the side to give Wheezer room to work.

The little dog secured the halter to a glum Bug. The contraption was loose but stayed put. He clipped the halter to the lead rope that was secured to the wagon.

"Let's go!" Cellar Cat said. Before hopping into the wagon, she slapped Bug's rump. He winced. "This'll be great."

"That should do it." Wheezer said.

He climbed into the cart and settled next to his new bestie, Cellar Cat. Their faces gleamed with anticipation. Bug frowned. If he hoped his friends saw how miserable he was and would forget about their game, he was mistaken.

"Lead on, trusty nag." Cellar Cat called out.

Disappointed, Bug pulled the wagon. Slowly at first, though not as a result of it being particularly heavy but because he wasn't sure of its durability. He imagined it falling apart with its riders aboard.

Cellar Cat spotted a long stick poking out of the grass. She snatched it up, and feeling impatient, proceeded to strike Bug's bottom with it. "Giddy-up, already!"

Though she only tapped him, Bug lunged forward as if he'd been walloped. His cheeks were soon flushed from exertion and his muscles ached. His concern for the wagon's stability increased with every step. Still, the pressure from the stick and the ridicule of his passengers pushed him onward.

With every tap, he picked up the pace. In no time he was jogging around the yard while his passengers whooped and hollered.

"F-faster, horsey!" howled Wheezer.

Once it sunk in that his friends were happy and enjoying themselves, Bug forgot about safety, discomfort or embarrassment and had fun too. Cellar Cat raised the stick in triumph, crying, "To the castle, loyal steed."

This time they all laughed. While Bug headed for the barn, he turned his head to enjoy his friends' laughter. But Cellar Cat had stopped laughing. Her mouth dropped and she pointed toward something in the distance. Bug knew what she was pointing at. Emmy had returned! Shifting his weight and squaring his body, he used every bit of might to pull the wagon away from the fence. He headed toward the protection of the woods at breakneck speed.

Bug heard her before he saw her. A ghastly snarl emanated from the brown blur as she gained on him and snapped at his back leg. He had tucked his tail as a baby fang grazed his hip. In a panic and with clouded vision, he hadn't realized that they entered the woods. Instead of slowing, he sped up. The wagon thumped along the rocky terrain hitting thick roots along the way. It swayed and swerved out of control. The nylon holding the rope to the wagon split. The halter loosened and slid down from Bug's forehead into his line of sight. He reduced speed but the wagon did not. The wheels slammed into the dog's back legs.

Wheezer and Cellar Cat, trying desperately to grab hold of the sides, were pitched from one end of the wagon to the other. Low bushes whipped at their faces and bodies.

The squeaks and squeals of the wagon combined with the caterwauling of its occupants cut through the peaceful woods. Bug heard Emmy snarling beside him and felt her hot breath on his shoulder. Disoriented, he lost his footing, slammed into Emmy's side and sent her sideways into a jungle of ferns. The bump caused the side of the wagon to careen into a tree. The rope snapped and Bug toppled forward, rolling into a thorny bush. Cellar Cat and Wheezer flew upward, colliding mid-air. She squeezed her scrawny arms around his bony neck, making his already bulbous eyes bigger.

She clung to him as they plunged feet first into a sandy embankment.

When the dust cleared, the moaning started. Cellar Cat, splayed out on her back, a paw draped over her forehead, meowed in pain. A groaning Wheezer rubbed his neck. Hidden by ferns and in the fetal position, Emmy yipped. Bug emerged from the thorny bush covered in thistles and bleeding. He squatted so as to not sit on a thorn and began pulling each sharp thistle out, ooohing and owing as he went. Cellar Cat watched him at first, then leaned in to carefully extract the ones Bug couldn't reach. With each thorn pulled came a fresh pang of guilt for how she had goaded him into being a horse.

"Is anybody hurt?" he asked as Cellar Cat removed the last thorn.

"My noggin!" Cellar Cat said, touching her head. She turned to where she'd last seen Emmy. "What were you trying to do, kill us?"

"Ouch." the chihuahua responded. She climbed out of the ferns, propped herself up on a tree stump, and held her wrist. Side-eyeing Bug, she said, "He's the one that stopped quick."
"I meant is anybody seriously hurt?" Bug said, making himself clear.
"No!" they replied at once.

"Alright, don't bite my head off."

"My neck hurts from being choked." Wheezer gaped at Cellar Cat.

"Nah." she said, examining his throat. "There's nothing there,weakling."

"No fighting, please." Bug took some deep breaths, stood up and observed the terrain. "Where are we? I can't see the farm."

The others, who seconds ago were only aware of their own suffering, now searched for some sense of familiarity. Bug and Cellar Cat turned to Wheezer, hoping he knew where they were. "I-I-I've never been in the woods." Wheezer wheezed. "I'm a couch potato."

"I go for walk-th all the time with the owners. There are a ton of winding paths. I don't recognize this one." Emmy said.
Cellar Cat threw up her paws and gave the chihuahua a challenging look. "Great! So, you're saying we're lost?"

Emmy growled. Cellar Cat hissed back. She faced an ocean and wasn't about to be intimidated by a tiny canine.

Wheezer rushed over, standing between the dog and cat, making an effort to diffuse the situation. "Stay calm."

Bug noted that the path they were on hand other trails branching off from it and found it impossible to tell which one they came from. "We're lost." he exclaimed. But no sooner had he said "No one panic." than everyone did.

"Oh, I'm panicking!" Cellar Cat screeched. "It's almost naptime! I haven't eaten! So, I suggest you get us out of here because I got a powerful hunger and am liable to eat one of you." She started toward a trail. "Do you think this is the way?"

She changed her mind. "Which way should I go?" she screamed. When no answer came, she said, "Ugh. I'm just going to have to pick one."

"I think we should stay here." Bug said patiently. "The owners will get worried and come looking for us."

"Wheezer said they'll be at a picnic. It'll be late before they realize we're gone. By then, we'll be impossible to find. I say we strike out ourselves."

That's when Emmy did something no one expected. Her face contorted into an awful grimace and she cried. They circled around her, astonished that something could be equal parts vicious and pitiful. Feeling self-conscious, she hid her face in the pads of her feet.

"Stop looking at me." she said.

Bug softened his voice. "It's ok to cry and be vulnerable. Vulnerability isn't weakness."

"Don't look at me, I said!"

Cellar Cat turned away. Embarrassed by the show of emotion. She grunted. With the goal of avoiding discomfort and finding home, she chose a trail. Without a second glance, she started down it.

"Cellar, we really should wait for help." Bug called.

"Wait for who?" She asked without turning. "I'm not sitting here. We'd all make a nice dinner for a pack of coyotes, don't ya think?"

She stomped on, her head held high. Bug stood motionless for a time, not wanting to leave but not wanting her to wander off alone either. Before she disappeared into the shadows, he chose his friend and raced to her side.

Wheezer plopped down where he stood, shouting, "I'm staying."

Emmy wiped away a tear and ran down the trail. "Don't leave me with him!" she whimpered.

The path the trio took went from flat and easy to rocky and difficult. After each bend Bug insisted, they turn back.

"There's a good chance we're more lost than ever." he'd say.

"We're going the right way. I can feel it." Cellar Cat kept repeating. "Just over this hill." But over every hill was more of the same.

"You guys are ridiculous. Where are we going?" She pointed to Bug's feet. "Can't your dumb little legs go any faster?"

Bug knew he was slowing them down. It had occurred to him that if he went back, the girls could get farther and faster without him. He also knew that Cellar Cat and Emmy couldn't stand each other. Every time one spoke, the other rolled her eyes. He hoped he could mediate their differences. He had faith that if they stayed together, using their individual strengths, they would

get back safely.

"I think we're going in circles. Emmy, you've got great eyesight, right?"

"Yep. So what?"

"With those peepers, how could she not?" laughed Cellar Cat. Bug ignored her.

"Could you keep your eyes out for ground markers? Anything that can easily be identified. That way if you see it again, we'll know we've been there before."

"I guess." She thought for a second. "I got a better idea." Stomping off to the nearest tree, she used her sharpest nail to carve an "X" in the trunk. "I'll mark the trees."

Impressed with her resourcefulness, Bug said, "Great thinking." Cellar Cat felt a tinge of jealousy. Not because Emmy had received a compliment but that the chihuahua had achieved respect for a trivial idea. The dog was mean one minute yet deserving of appreciation the next. The cat thought of her behavior in the last hours. They were more alike than she hoped.

Emmy fully committed to her job. As they walked, she marked every fifth or sixth tree. This meant she trailed behind, giving Cellar Cat the chance to speak freely. "Why are you being nice to the beastie? She's means to you."

"For one, you're not always nice to me, and for another, we want to work together toward a common goal—in this case, getting home. We have to be civil. Plus, we don't know what's going on with her. I'm not excusing her behavior. She's responsible for it, but she could be hurting. I'd rather cooperate together than hurt her. Besides, she's cute. How could anyone be mean to that face?"

"I can." Cellar Cat picked up a rock, throwing it deep into the woods. "You know, you don't have to be a goody-goody all the time. Stand up for yourself. Don't let her push you around."

"That's rich coming from you. Being a good leader means modeling good behavior. I can protect myself and lead at the same time. She's not pushing me around. In case you didn't notice, she's being helpful."

The cat stopped herself from blurting out further criticism of Emmy for fear of exposing her own bad conduct.

"Leading isn't telling others what to do—it's working with them to get everyone's needs met in some way." Bug looked thoughtful.
"It's stressful, actually."

"Hmmm, why don't you use your stress-aids then?" Cellar Cat stuck her tongue out at him. She meant it in a playful way but he remained serious.

"I am. Please don't make this harder for me. I'm trying my best to manage the situation."

"Speaking of the devil, here she comes now." Cellar Cat murmured.
"What are you dummies whispering about?"
"We dummy are looking for the smartest way out of here." said the cat. The little dog marked another tree.

After an hour of trudging in the sweltering sun, Emmy shrieked, "Guys, guys, we've been here before. Look!" She pointed to a tiny x low on a tree root.

"Oh!" Cellar Cat, dramatically, collapsed to the forest floor.

"Ok. Ok." Bug held up his arm. "At least we know now. Thanks, Emmy. Great job."

Emmy stood razor sharp, nodding her chin.

"What are we going to do, Bozo?" asked Cellar Cat.

"We brainstorm. Any suggestions?"

"No. It's getting late, and I'm all out of ideas. We're going to be stuck here forever."

"That's the opposite of helpful, Cellar." Bug said. "Your nighttime vision means you can keep an eye out for danger."

"Oh my gosh, I forgot about coyotes. What other predators are here? We talking bears? Wolves? Lions?"

"Are you kidding? There are no lions in Maine."

"How should I know! I'm a city cat."

"Wait!" Emmy piped in. "I've got it. Today is the Fourth of July. Why didn't I think of this before?"

"So what?" Cellar Cat said pointedly. Emmy snarled back.

"Every Fourth of July my owner sets off fireworks."

"What do you want—a medal? Yeesh."

Bug sprung up, tail wagging. "Don't you see? The fireworks will be visible from here. We'll follow them back to the farm. Brilliant, Emmy!"

Emmy, held her head high.

"Hallelujah." breathed Cellar Cat. "What do we do till then?"

"We wait." Bug dropped down in the shade of a pine tree. Emmy sat beside him. "You keep an eye out for danger while we rest." he said to Cellar Cat.

She sighed. It wasn't fair. She wanted to relax too. In truth, though, she was too anxious about circling coyotes to rest. She was torn between hating responsibility and not wanting to let the Bug down. Since he was right and she did have the best vision of the bunch, she dutifully patrolled the area, her eyes darting left, right and back again.

The sun faded and the forest cooled. Refreshed and clear-headed, Bug guesstimated their location by using a stick to make a map in the dirt while Emmy kept an eye on the sky for fireworks.

"This trip has been the worst." Cellar Cat said.

"I think it's been great." said Bug.

"Have we been on the same trip?"

"It's been challenging but still fun."

"Huh?"

"Every challenge is an opportunity to grow. Look how much stronger we've become!"

"You're impossible."

"You mean I just got stronger?" Emmy chimed in, taking her eyes off the sky for a moment.

"Yup." Bug answered.

She studied her scrawny arms. "How?"

"Not physical strength." Bug said. "Inner strength."

"Oh." She sat for a time, thinking. "You're saying that every time I do my best, I get stronger in my mind?"

"Uh-huh. Small at first, but if you push past your comfort zone one step every day, the change is drastic."

Emmy's mouth hung open and her already large eyes widened. "Really?"

"This morning you've learned how to work as a team and shared your ideas to benefit the group. That's drastic."

"I do feel tougher."

"You can be scary with brute force or you can be truly frightening by strengthening your mind."

"I can be both!" Emmy said.

Cellar Cat groaned. "Now you've done it. If her head gets any bigger, she'll topple over."

A sudden loud crack followed by a deafening eruption thundered above. The dark sky lit up in bursting color. The display rattled the group, but upon realizing what it was, they clapped.

"Fireworks!" they whooped.

A shower of rainbow light radiated across their happy faces.

"Well, let's go." Cellar Cat said, no longer interested in the spectacle.

"I know the way. Follow me." Emmy, her ears flapping, galloped toward the fireworks.

Bug and Cellar Cat trailed her to the boundary of the grand-people's yard. Emmy waited by the fence for her new friends to catch up.

"My owner will be sooo happy to see me." She leaned in close to Bug and whispered, "Sorry about this morning. I thought you were going to make fun of my cute-neth. Most do. But you're ok. By the way, that cat shouldn't call you Bozo." The last bit she said loud enough for Cellar Cat to hear. That a naughty thing like Emmy would say that made the cat think about why she still called him that. It had become a nickname but she understood now that it was hurtful.

Just before scrambling under the fence, Emmy waved and called, "See ya later, suckers." Bug waved back.

Cellar Cat said, "I, for one, am glad to see the back of that dog."

"I liked her."

"You would."

Bug pointed at the farmhouse. "We gotta go rally the owners. Wheezer is still out there."

A firework burst forward, illuminating the porch. There, seated casually on the front step, was Wheezer. They raced to him.

"How'd you get back?" Bug asked.

"I used my nose."

Cellar Cat gave Bug a thump on the back. "Why didn't you do that, Boz...I mean Bug?" He turned pink.
"Oops. I forgot about my sniffer."

"Hey, wait a minute. When did you get here? Were you going to just leave us out there for the lions?"

"There's no lions, Cellar, I just got back now. The owners aren't even home."

"Sure, sure." She put an arm around Bug's shoulder and directed him toward the door. "C'mon, let's get some grub." She scowled at Wheezer. "No fibbers allowed."

"I-I'm not fibbing!"

"Yeah, yeah, tell it to the lions. Right now, I'm all about food and shuteye."

Wheezer was right: the house was empty. He explained that his owners were usually gone long into the night. The group stole into the kitchen for a dinner of kibble that had been left out for them. With full bellies, they returned to the porch. Cellar Cat and Wheezer nodded off as soon as their heads hit their beds. The cat dreamed of blue skies and summer adventures with her new friends. Wheezer had a nightmare about a cow trying to stomp his tail. Bug, with a tender expression, watched the last firework fizzle out. He made a friend, it was a good day.

Three days later they were packed up in their crates and headed for home. They spent the first leg of the ride reliving their adventures and laughing over the funny bits but as the drive dragged on, Cellar Cat picked fights over minor details. She insisted their goodbyes went as follows: Wheezer bowed down to kiss her paw, Emmy waved enthusiastically from her fence and Bumbles saluted her. Bug maintained that none of that was true.

"Wheezer barked his farewell, Emmy sulked from her fence holes, and Bumbles never made an appearance." They bickered the rest of the trip. They even argued as they were being lifted out of the back of the car and while their crates were being pulled from the backyard to the basement. By the time they were set free, they weren't speaking.

Later that day, while Bug gnawed on a bone, Cellar Cat gingerly walked over to him.

"Ok, I may have exaggerated a smidge. Happy now?"

"Yeah. Why lie, though?"

She shrugged. "I'm not sure exactly, but I think I know." She was ready to tell Bug about her Mom.

"I'm all ears." He wiggled his ears to prove his point.

"Well...I was born here. My mom was a stray that found a way into the basement. She had my sister and me in that corner there." She pointed to a spot under the stairs.

"Awwww, kittens. You had a sister?"

"Uh-huh. Anyway, when I was about two weeks old, the owners almost found us. My mom went

137

with my sister to a safe spot but never came back for me. She promised to but didn't." The cat teared up. "The woman bottle fed me. I almost didn't survive. Later, Dr. Lee said that the early separation from my mom was the reason I am, quote "terribly bratty." Her exact words."

"That's awful." Bug patted her paw with his. "Thanks for telling me. It explains a lot. But like with Emmy, even if things are tough, you're still responsible for your actions."

"I know that now. Seeing her behave that way made me see my own bad behavior. I guess that's why I didn't like Emmy. I saw myself in her." She stomped her foot and said, "I'm going to try to do better."

"And I admit that I'm not always a good friend. I can be bossy and judgy." Bug said shyly.

"Thanks, but I'm going to own my mistakes from now on."

"What can I do to help?"

"Nothing. It's up to me." She lifted her chin. "Don't expect miracles." Bug rolled his bone toward her.
"Ewwww. Is that your idea of a peace offering?"

"Yup. It's tasty. Try it."

"No, thank you. I'll stick with kitty yum yums."

Cellar Cat felt closer to Bug. She had been through a great deal in the last two weeks and he had been by her side every step of the way.

"Hey, I really liked playing king of the castle—err, wagon—didn't you? Before the accident, I mean."Said the cat.
"Yeah."
This gave Bug an idea. He found a rope, fed it through the tabs at either end of his dog bed, took

the ends in his mouth, then shimmied himself in front of the bed.

"Climb aboard," he spluttered through the rope ends. Cellar Cat giggled as she hopped onto the bed.

For the rest of the evening he galloped around the basement pulling her behind him. During a break, much to Bug's horror, Cellar Cat found a stick, but instead of using it like a switch to smack his rear, she used it as a makeshift sword. She held it up in victory and shouted, "Onward, brave steed!"

It was even better than the king of the wagon.

BABIES

"Do you smell that?" Cellar Cat asked the next day. She sniffed and snuffed the air as Bug unpacked his things.

"Nope."

"I swear your nose doesn't work."

"It's slow is all."

Bug carefully put his belongings away while Cellar Cat busied herself trying to ignore the stench. It got to the point where it overwhelmed her senses.

"It's a familiar odor. Not a good one, either."

"There's a chance that I left food out. Sometimes I fall asleep while eating and when I wake up it's gone. I'm saying, it's possible that I sleep eat."

"No such thing."

"Well, food could roll under the washing machine, those chests of drawers or the dryer. Who knows? But if I lost it before the trip, it'd be ripe."

"I'm telling you, it's not food." She sat down to mull it over. "A rat. Yeah, I'm sure of it. That's an odor I picked up on the boat."

"A rat! I hope not. There were rats in the shelter when I was a pup. They came out at night. If I slept too deeply, I'd wake to them chewing my tail. I have scars. Emotional and physical."

"The odor is coming from over there." Cellar Cut crept toward the old chest of drawers under the stairs. Upon further inspection, she

found a drawer ajar and after a sniff, she took a giant leap back.

"Oh man! It's in there for sure. Phew."

"What should we do?"

"You check it out. Rats are gross." she said.

"Ok. I-I'm not afraid." Bug stammered. "I'm bigger now. If it tries to bite me, I'll knock its block off." He steadied himself. "Deep breaths. Bug, you can do this."

He timidly peered into the drawer then let out a silent gasp. The worry lines that had gathered around his eyelids diminished.

"Awww." He breathed a sigh of relief.

"What is it?" Cellar Cat asked loudly.

He pointed to the drawer. "Shh. See for yourself."

Curious, Cellar Cat peeked over the edge of the drawer. Curled up inside a nest of dryer lint were two tiny mice. Bug's eyes blazed forth like candle flames. "Babies."

"Yuck." Cellar Cat sauntered off.

"You don't want to eat them?"

"Gross. I have kitty kibble. Besides, they smell. Rotten little things." She held her nose. "Blech."

"I don't smell anything."

"You wouldn't."

Bug brushed off the insult.

"Let's keep them. I wonder where their mother is."

"What? No. I won't eat 'em, but you've got to get rid of them. I can't stand the smell. Anyhow, if the owners find any evidence of mice they'll set out traps. You don't want headless babies running around, do you?"

"No! No!"

"Then get rid of them."

"But I can't. Just look. So small and fragile. They wouldn't survive out there on their own. If their mom comes back, I'll warn her of the danger, but I'm not kicking them out into that cruel world."

Cellar Cat thought of how her Mom never came back. Her chest felt heavy. "Whatever, it's their funeral."

Bug rested his head on the edge of the drawer, content to watch them sleep, but eventually his hot breath woke them. Eyes closed, they stretched. When they gently opened them and saw his big ogling face, they froze.

"Hello, little ones. Don't worry, I won't harm you." he said softly.

They exhaled and wiggled their noses. Though they couldn't see Cellar Cat from the drawer, they smelled her.

"Pay no attention to Cellar. She may look mean but it's all show."

"I could eat them if I wanted to." she said from across the room. "I have the teeth for it." The babies shuttered.
"She won't either. I'll make sure of it."

The cat harrumphed.

"Where is your momma?" he asked...

"We don't know." They squeaked in unison. They unfurled themselves. One was small and thin. the other tall with a protruding belly. The bigger one spoke.
"She left to get food two days ago but hasn't come back." Cellar Cat felt her heart skip a beat.
"Oh, I'm sorry. I'm sure she'll come back. Are you hungry?" Asked Bug "That's a stupid question, of course you are. I'll get food."

147

Bug ran up to the kitchen and returned with a pocket-size buffet of fruit, cheese, and cracker bits on a coaster. The mice ate with gusto.

"Thank you, thank you." they said after they'd eaten. The babies yawned and promptly fell back to sleep.

While they slept, Bug searched for items to make a larger, comfier mouse bed. He filled an old cigar box with bits he thought a mother mouse might use: remnants of fabric, yarn and cotton from the owner's sewing kit, dryer lint from the wastebasket and a worry doll he found under the upstairs couch cushions. He hoped it would make a nice doll for them.

He presented the cigar box bed to Cellar Cat. "Do you think they'll like it?"

"Don't care." she said, sharpening her nails on the back of the sofa.

Bug frowned. Seeing his disappointment, she added, "I'm sure it's fine."

"I want to make sure they're happy until their momma comes back."

Deep frown lines formed on her forehead.

"I hate to rain on your sentimental parade, Bug, but she ain't coming back."

"Of course, she is. Why say such a thing?"

"You can be so naive. Doesn't matter. They're your problem, not mine."

"If she doesn't come back—and I'm not saying she won't—I'm going to take care of them. They're newborns."

"Ick. Suit yourself. I won't have anything to do with them. Like I said, it's dangerous here. Don't cry me a river when you're cleaning up their tiny bobble heads off the carpet."

"Don't say that! They might hear you!" Realizing he was yelling, he whispered, "I'll keep them safe." Moving to the stairs, he added, "Watch them while I get them a snack."
"Yeah. No." Cellar Cat climbed up on one of the high-back chairs. "Were you listening to me?"

"Ok. Ok." With belly rumbling, Bug stood watch over the mice. "Snacks can wait."

Later that day, the baby mice became restless. Bug nuzzled them with his nose. They squealed with laughter. Once they were fully awake, he presented them with their new bed. They showed their appreciation by doing zoomies all around it.

Two days past and there was still no sign of the mom. The babies took to following Bug everywhere. He learned that the bigger mouse was a boy named Little Fat Tummy.

"I named myself 'cause look at this fine, full belly." He jiggled his paunch with his paws. The smaller mouse was a girl named Soda.
"My ma names me on accounts of me being bubbly," she said.

Soda in particular, became attached to Bug. She rode everywhere on his back and called him "Buggy Pops," which made his heart swell.
Although Cellar Cat tried to act indifferent, she noted that she'd never seen Bug so content, particularly during their bedtime routine. Bug

would gently rough-house with Little Fat Tummy while Soda cheered on her "Buggy Pops." Then he'd lay flat on the floor while the babies climbed all over him like a jungle gym. Next, he'd sit, with the most serene look while the mice took turns using his back as a slide. Starting at the crown of his head, they'd slide all the way down, screaming with delight the entire way down.

Finally, he'd say "Alright, little ones, bedtime."

Despite their protests, he'd carry the mice to their soft cigar box bed. There were many hugs and kisses back and forth while tucking them in. At the end of the day, he'd collapse in his own bed, exhausted.

"The rascals." he'd say dreamily.

The babies grew fast and by summer's end were zooming all over the basement. Bug felt it was important to introduce safety rules.

"One: no going upstairs. If the owners suspect there's mice here, they will set traps. Two: no bothering Cellar. I'm not saying she'll eat you; I'm not saying she won't."

"And three: under no circumstances do you go to the backyard. There are dangers everywhere."

Bug had confidence in Soda. She was trustworthy and disciplined. Little Fat Tummy, on the other hand, was headstrong and adventurous. A rule-breaker. Bug often caught him creeping up the stairs or sneaking toward Cellar Cat while she slept. The dog's biggest concern was how the mouse was preoccupied with the doggie door leading to the yard. Bug spent many sleepless nights worrying about the horrible things that could happen to them out in the world.

"Stop fretting." Cellar Cat would say. "They're just mice. Besides, they're almost grown. They mature faster than us. At some point, you'll have to prepare them for the world. They can't stay cooped up forever. You saw what happened to me. I'm much happier now that I conquered my fear of the outside."

"I'd like to keep them safe as long as I can." He'd respond.

One afternoon his fears came to be. Bug awoke to discover the mice missing. He remained calm, calling out to them, searching their hidey holes. But when he couldn't find them, panic set in. He barked while ransacking the basement. He pulled cushions off the sofa and chairs, opened drawers, flipped pet beds, and dumped the wastebasket. Seeing his distress, Cellar Cat searched for them too. Eventually she tracked their scent to the door.

"They must've gone outside. Sorry."

"No. They wouldn't." Bug lowered his head. "Why would they?" His expression was a mix of disappointment, anger and devastation.

"Don't take it personally. They're young and curious."

Her words had no effect. Bug followed her out to the backyard. She chased the scent to the swan gate where she lost it. The dog slumped down and cried.

"They left the yard?" He croaked. Long tendrils of snot dribbled from his nose.

155

"Don't give up, yet." Cellar Cat tried to sound optimistic. She wasn't very good at it.

She sat on a sun-soaked rock to think. She remembered that when she had gone missing Bug asked Squirrelly for help. He knew everything that went on in the neighborhood, so she called to him.

"Hey, Squirrel-lee, come here."
No response. She was at a loss for what to do next because Bug's sobbing had become increasingly noisy and she couldn't focus. But soon there came a chattering from above. The crying had drawn Squirrelly's attention.
"Help." was all Cellar Cat said. She hoped he understood her as didn't speak squirrel.

Squirrelly looked from the dog to the cat and shrugged.

"Mice missing. Need help. Find?" she said.

No response. The cat didn't know what to do. She needed Bug to talk to the squirrel, but at the moment he was inconsolable. Useless, she thought. Why was she responsible for mice she didn't even want in the first place? Being in charge of someone else's problem wasn't her thing.

"How about this? Find Bug's mice, stupid squirrel, or face the consequences. Is that clear enough?" The squirrel pointed at her, chattered something with a clenched fist and leapt away. Cellar Cat went to Bug's side. "Squirrelly will find them." She wasn't sure if he heard but he cried a little less loudly.

A half-hour later, when Squirrelly reappeared, he spoke only to Bug.

157

He talked fast and skittered away as quickly as he came. Cellar Cat wasn't sure what was said but it clearly wasn't good news. Bug whimpered and rocked as he blubbered that Squirrelly hadn't heard a thing. They were tiny after all. The squirrel did ask his network to keep looking. Squirrelly then pledged to update them if there was any news.

"That doesn't mean anything bad happened. The babies are probably somewhere close. Sitting here won't do any good. Let's go take a nap. All this responsibility is making me tired."
Bug let out an ear-splitting wail.

She sighed, understanding that she'd been selfish."Ok, ok. Do you want to go look for them?" He nodded.

"I thought good dogs don't wander."

The rims of his eyes were swollen pink. "There are exceptions."

The pair scoured the neighborhood. They asked any fenced pets, strays, and dogs on leashes if they had seen the mice. No luck. A gang of overenthusiastic street cats requested detailed descriptions of the babies so they might seek them out themselves. Bug almost fainted. Cellar Cat shooed them away.

Across the street from their backyard and behind a tall chain-link fence, Bug and Cellar Cat met two dogs—Marina, a shaggy black mix, and Louisa, a Boxer with a protruding lower jaw. Louisa took immediate interest in their plight. Marina, however, scoffed at them. She explained that mice had bad vibes and Cellar Cat's chakras needed clearing.

"You'll help?" Bug asked Louisa. It was the first spark of energy he'd had since his babies went missing. He looked up at the high fence. "But how?"

"Easy." said Louisa.

She pushed the gate while lifting the latch with her muzzle. The gate swung open.

 "Amazing!" said Bug.

"She's an escape artist." Marina called from the other end of the yard. "Leave it ajar for me. I'm going to Pierre's to trade our leftover breakfast for a few crystals and some incense."

Louisa turned her chin toward a junkyard two doors down. "Pierre is our neighbor. His owner is a hoarder. If you need anything, he can get it for you in a pinch."

"Good to know. Thanks." Bug said. "Can he get us information on the missing mice?"

"I doubt it." Marina barked.

Louisa mentioned that she had a decent nose and offered to track the mice. They returned to their backyard for her to pick up the scent.

"It ends here." Cellar Cat pointed between the sidewalk and the swan gate. "Let me try. Sometimes I smell things other animals don't." A branch snapped above them. They looked up. "Hey there, Squirrelly." Louisa said with a smile. He waved back then bounded off.
"You know Squirrelly? Is that his name?" Bug asked excitedly.

"Sure, anyone that takes the time to listen to him knows his name and he's nice to know if you lost something."
Bug glanced at Cellar. "Told ya."
While Louisa combed the area for a scent, Bug explained to Cellar Cat the art of communicating with Squirrelly. She couldn't have cared less

about talking to a dimwitted squirrel but she feigned interest because it kept Bug's mind busy. "It's a series of chirps, chatters, small words and gestures. But you have to be pleasant." He emphasized pleasant. "Otherwise you'll be ignored or insulted. He won't be disrespected." "Got it!" Louisa called from the sidewalk.

Bug clapped. "Goodie! Lead the way."

They followed Louisa for twenty-five minutes. First to the outskirts of their block leading to a rundown neighborhood. Next was a steep incline to a busy intersection and a commercial road full of chain restaurants and strip malls.
Upon entering the booming inner city, Cellar Cat was inclined to spring at every horn and siren. Her last experience outside the neighborhood wasn't positive and her instinct told her to go home. Instead, she moved forward, concentrating on a positive outcome for her

162

friend. The cat kept between Bug and the concrete buildings for protection. The towering skyscrapers made her feel small and insignificant. It was a feeling she was unfamiliar with.

"Oh, dear! Why would they come here?" Bug exclaimed. He seemed ruffled by their surroundings.

Tracking was slowed due to the overlapping odors on the sidewalks. The mingled stench of cigarette butts, globs of chewing tobacco, discarded food, stinky shoes and other trash that littered the streets impaired Louisa's ability to isolate the mice's scent. While she nosed around, Bug paced.

"How did they get this far? I hope they're ok. Such little things alone in a big city!"

"They'll be ok. They're small but tough." said Cellar Cat.

"No, they're softies. They only act tough. Look at me. I'm bigger than them but I was terrified every time I was dropped off at a pound— and I had walls and a fence to protect me from the city."

"Geesh, how many times were you surrendered?"

"Four."

Cellar Cat couldn't hide her shock. Maybe a few months ago she would have understood a human not wanting a canine, but now she was dumbfounded as to why any person would give up on a nice dog like Bug.

"You'd think I'd get used to it but I never did." he said "The second time was the worst. There were three girls in my family and I was with them for three years. I was the first to greet the youngest at the door when she came home as a newborn and I slept by her crib every night." His lip trembled. "I loved them so much and I thought they loved me and was sure it was my forever home but..." he stared off into the distance. "I became a burden, I guess."

Cellar Cat felt his sorrow in her bones.

"That's lousy." Wanting to change the subject so as to not compound his suffering, she asked, "What's the pound like?"

He narrowed his eyes. "It's the worst. Stinky, loud, lonely. Some, like my mentor, Daisy, never left. Next time I'll be going to the room for sure. No one will want me. Too old."

"Stop." She put her paw on his. "You're not going back."

"I've pretty much accepted the fact that that's where I'll end up. Alone, in one of those rooms."

"That's where it leads." It was Louisa directing them toward an alleyway.

Even in the bright light of day the alley was dark and ominous; a dead end of overflowing garbage bags and scavenged trash. They meandered around the bags looking for clues.

"Reeks of alleycat." said the boxer.

"Oh, my poor babies!" Bug squawked. "That's it. They're gone. I failed as a mouse parent. You were right all along, Cellar. I'm pathetic."

"C'mon, that's not true. I was mean when I said that. You were a great mouse parent. Bad things happen and sometimes no one's to blame."

"Why did they leave then? 'Cause I'm not good enough, that's why. That's why everyone leaves me."

"Stop feeling sorry for yourself! That gets you nowhere but a fast track to bitterness. You are many things but you are not bitter. They are almost grown and needed to explore. It happens. True, it's not the best ending, but you did nothing wrong." She sidled over to him, leaning against his side. "And just so you know, I won't leave you, ever."

It was then that she heard a sound. A familiar one, barely perceptible by anyone other than a cat. It pricked her ears. The scratching of plastic. She heard it before, at home, upstairs in the wastebasket. It was coming from inside a garbage bag. Recognizing what it was, she padded over and slashed the bag open. The contents tumbled out. Oxidized soda cans, used diapers, wet napkins, empty to-go containers, a moldy Styrofoam box and a soggy dark ball that spun to Bug's feet.

It squeaked as it unrolled itself to reveal a twitching nose and long whiskers. "Soda!" Bug shrieked.

"Buggy Pops!" the baby mouse chirped.

He scooped her up. She was shivering, covered in slime, and smelled of rancid food but was otherwise unharmed. He smooched her head while dancing a jig down the alleyway. She hugged him with her tiny toes.

Bug beamed at Louisa and bowed. "You found her! Thank you." She bowed back.

Holding Soda close to his chest, he scanned the area. "Where's Tummy?"

"I don't know. Some bigs dog drags hims away in its mouths. I escape by hidings in here."

Bug trembled, but for Soda's sake, tried to show no outward concern.

"You were brave. I'm proud of you, little one."

On the hike back home, Soda rode on Bug's back. She explained that she left the basement to convince her brother to return. He had found a fingerboard outside the swan gate and persuaded her to hop aboard. They immediately lost control and the skateboard took them to the city. They found an alley, heard a gang of cats caterwauling, and hid in the garbage behind a tin can. Next thing she knew a dog barked and Little Fat Tummy screamed. Tears streamed from Bug's cheeks to the concrete. Cellar Cat was at a loss for words. She gave him the occasional sympathetic smile, but it did little to lift his spirits. It was dark when they reached their street. The cat thanked Louisa, who trotted toward her yard. Bug dragged his feet to the swan gate where he sat heavily at its entry. Soda slid down.

"Buggy Pops, I's going to gets some waters." He composed himself. She gave him a peck on his wet cheek before running into the house.

"We'll be in in a minute." Cellar Cat called.

Once Soda was out of sight, Bug slumped over. His eyes dissolved into brown puddles. Cellar Cat tried to lift him up but wasn't strong enough.

"Let's go in, it's getting late."

They trudged through the gate. Cellar Cat turned to close the latch and noticed Louisa across the street, jumping up and down on her fence. She was waving frantically with one paw while pointing at Marina with the other.

"Something's going on over at Louisa's." The cat said.

Bug didn't hear or care. He lumbered toward the doggie door. The cat squinted. Another dog joined Louisa. A short French bulldog jumped beside her. They both began to bark.
"Bug, Louisa wants us."
"I-I can't."

"Maybes she's heard somethings." squeaked Soda. She had returned and was watching Bug intently.

"You go ahead." he said.

"No. It could be important. You're coming." said the cat.

"Comes on, Pops. You can't give up nows."

171

The hope in Soda's voice stirred something in Bug. He composed himself and cleared his throat. "You're right, little one."

They paraded across the bumpy cobblestone to the brick sidewalk on the opposite side of the street where Louisa and the bulldog still bounced excitedly. Marina was behind them with her mouth full. Something long and pink hung from her lips.

"Look at that." Cellar Cat pointed out. "She's drooling. Dogs are slobs. Eww."

"That's tails." Soda squealed in horror. "A mouse tails!"

"She's eating a mouse?" Cellar Cat asked.

The tail in Marina's mouth wriggled.

"It's Little Fat Tummy!" Bug shouted.

He ran toward Marina and bared his teeth. "Drop him." His voice was hard and angry. Louisa raised her foot in protest.

"Slow down. It's ok," she said. "Marina found him and brought him back. She's a better tracker than I am. She used to be a hunting dog. After we left, she felt guilty about refusing to help, but we were already miles down the road." Marina nodded as Louisa continued. "She found them in the alley and caught Little Fat Tummy right away, but not Soda. Don't worry, Tummy is unharmed."

"Tummy?" asked Cellar Cat.

"That's what he wants to be called." grunted the Frenchie. Saliva dribbled from Marina's mouth.

"Teenage stuff. Anyway, Tummy kept running off to try to find you. She had to contain him somehow." Louisa nodded to Marina. "You can let him out now."

Marina lowered her head, opened her mouth, and carefully pushed the slobbery mouse out with her tongue. Coming from a hot mouth, Tummy shivered in the cool air.

"Ohhhh, my boy!" said Bug.

Tummy's first reaction was to put his fists up to Marina but once he saw everyone smiling at him, he ran to Bug, wrapped his wet wiry arms around Bug's leg and buried himself there. Mucus oozed from the mouse's armpits. Love emitted from every pore in Bug's body.

A tear formed in Cellar Cat's eye. She wiped it away.

"Sorry, Buggy Pops. I won't never leave again." Tummy squeezed Bug tighter.

"I'm glad you're alright." blubbered Bug. He picked up the mouse. "I was overprotective. There will still be rules, but you shouldn't be cooped up all the time. You can go in the backyard with me, and I can even sneak you upstairs once in a while when the owners are out."

Cellar Cat knew that her friend had been overwhelmed with the babies, and if they had worked together as they had in Maine, maybe the mice wouldn't have left.

"From now on, if you don't follow the rules, you'll have to contend with me, right, Bug?" she said, winking at him.

Bug winked back. "That's right, Aunty Cellar."

To her surprise, she didn't hate the sound of that.

Bug turned to the hero of the hour. " Thank you, Marina. I don't know what to say."

"Actually, I'd like to apologize, man. After consulting the Tarot cards, I realized that I was being judgmental, so I went to search for your kids. Like Louisa said, I'm a good tracker. Once I get a scent, I don't lose it."

The French bulldog, Pierre, stepped forward to introduce himself and invite everyone to his yard for lunch the next day. All but Marina accepted the invitation. She said she'd be busy teaching a yoga class at the local chipmunk association.

"Speaking of lunch, let's go home. I'm hungry." said Cellar Cat.

Not waiting for the others, she bolted for the swan gate hollering, "Race ya home! Last one there's a rotten tomato!"

BYE BUG

"I love falls."

Bug nudged a pile of fallen leaves in the backyard.

The hot summer months were replaced by cool days and brisk nights. The leaves turned and were either blazing forth from the trees or plummeting to earth with graceful flair. Cellar Cat and Bug waded through the crunchy leaves while taking their morning walk.

"Not me. I don't have enough bulk to keep me warm." said the cat. She was shivering and impatient to get back inside.

"I got plenty." Bug said with a chuckle.

The sun was a dim yellow sphere in a bleary white sky. Streets and sidewalks were a kaleidoscope of rich orange, yellow, and red foliage. A biting wind lifted and swirled the leaves. The crisp air tickled Bug's nose and chilled his skin. He thought about how much had changed since summer. They had new friends in Marina, Louisa and Pierre, the weather had turned and the mice were full-grown. Though Soda stayed in the same drawer in the bed Bug had made, Tummy moved to a large box in the farthest corner of the basement. They still spent some time with Aunty Cellar and Buggy Pops, but they had separate lives with their own friends.

"They grow fast. It's gone by in a heartbeat." Bug said with a sigh.

"I told you they would."

Cellar Cat thought of recent changes too. Although it had only been a couple of months, Bug looked and acted as if he'd aged years. His white muzzle was now gray, and he was slower and stiffer. He tried to hide the hurt but Cellar Cat could see him straining with each step. Getting up and down was particularly difficult. He played and ate less, slept and stumbled more.

"It's nothing." he'd say when he'd fall, but she couldn't help but worry.

There were other things too, like forgetfulness and confusion. He couldn't recall names, times or events. His recollection was hazy and he often forgot his friends. It took only a reminder from Cellar Cat for his memory to return, but it still concerned her, especially since it seemed to worsen weekly. He had long since lost his pocket-sized stuffed bunny. Even his navy-blue collar with silver dog tags would go missing from time to time—the collar was, above all else, his most cherished possession. It meant he had a home. The fact that Bug regularly lost it alarmed the cat.

They're late afternoon walk led them to Pierre's for some shopping. He was a sturdy old fellow who snorted non-stop. He was patient with Bug's short memory and often guided him along his wares. They had become buddies and would spend hours talking about old times.

Cellar Cat was examining a new cardboard box for Little Fat Tummy. His had fallen apart at the seams. She aggressively bargained for the box with Pierre while Bug searched for something special, though he couldn't remember what.

"Whatever it is, it's small." he said.

He examined a twisted jumble of costume jewelry laid out on a blanket.

"No, these are not what I'm looking for." A raindrop tapped his nose. He took no notice.

"Shiny. What are they?" he asked.

Cellar Cat sighed. "Jewelry. Earrings and necklaces. Remember, the owner wears them all the time."

"Ohhh. But what are they for?"

"Adornment. Like collars." She noticed that he wasn't wearing his. "Bug, you forgot your collar again."

"Huh, is that right?"

"Not a good day for that." Said Pierre. "The animal control officer is making his rounds. Went up the street twenty minutes ago and is due back soon. Best to make yourself scarce," snuffed Pierre, touching his own collar. "This officer asks no questions. No collar? It's the shelter. He's a tough one."

"What's a shelter?" Bug asked.

Cellar Cat opened her mouth to explain but thought it better not to remind him. Some things are best forgotten.

A sudden sprinkling resulted in Pierre hurriedly packing his merchandise.

"We better get home." Cellar Cat moved to get the dog, but he caught sight of Marina next door. "Hello." he called. Cellar Cat waved. The rain pelted her lashes.

Bug climbed on the chain-link fence. Rain plinked off the fence onto his face.

"Have we met?" he asked, wagging his tail.

"Yes. It's Marina." the cat reminded him.

Marina woofed a greeting just as the animal control car cruised past. The bark caught the officer's attention. Marina and Pierre, who had noticed the vehicle stop, howled warnings to their friends.

Cellar Cat spun in time to see the officer get out of his car, but Bug, muddled by the mixture of raindrops and noisy barking, had not.

"Bug, come quickly!" she said.

Her words came too late. In mere seconds, the man had checked for a collar and seeing none, scooped up the dog and threw him, rather harshly, into a cage in the back of the cruiser.

Bug yelped in pain. Not knowing what else to do, she clung to the officer's pant leg, pleading with the man to release Bug.

"Please. He has a home. He forgot his collar. I'll show you."

"Meow, meow, meow, meow." was what the officer heard.

He dropped to his knees and took hold of the small tag on her collar.

"You've got an owner. Go home."

The officer rose, got into his vehicle, and sped away just as it began to downpour. Cellar Cat couldn't move.
"Bye Bug," she mouthed in a daze as the car disappeared around the corner.

One minute he was beside her; the next he was gone, snatched up and on his way to some shelter. The shelter! Oh no, she thought. The place he dreaded most.

He must feel frightened, confused, abandoned. Last time he spoke of it, he said he'd end up in the "room." The cat wept as she imagined his panic. Her only hope was that his memory failed him and he wouldn't recall past experiences there. Marina and Pierre made every effort to console her, but it was no good. The best thing that ever happened to her would soon be locked up in a pound downtown. While the world moved in slow-motion, her mind was chaos.

She'd never see him again. He'd spend his last minutes of his life alone in the Room. She'd never again hear his slow voice or listen to his unsolicited advice. Wasn't there anybody who could save him? The owners, maybe. No. By the time they realized he was gone; it'd be too late.

He was doomed. She felt herself disintegrate into the sidewalk.

And that's when a voice inside her told her Bug needed her. If their roles were reversed, he wouldn't give up on her. He'd do something. It occurred to her that the reason Bug had allowed himself to be vulnerable when the mice went missing was because he trusted her to find a solution. But what could she do now? She was just a cat. What is a cat, though, if not resourceful, cunning, clever? She was all those things and more. That's why Bug loved her. When the mice went missing, she took charge. Bug trusted her.

She arched her neck, holding an outstretched fist toward the drizzling sky.

"I'll get Bug out of there. With every bit of strength, I have. And when I get him out, as god is my witness, he'll never go back there again." The determination she felt wasn't strengthened by anger, vanity, or ego, but by love. She was stronger and more certain than she ever had been before. She wasn't going back home without him. The basement, which, a short time ago, seemed cramped and inconvenient with him would now be quiet and lonely without him.

"It'd be easier with help, though." She turned to see Pierre, Louisa and Marina watching her.

"Are you alright?" said Louisa, who had come out just as Cellar Cat finished her speech.

"Yes. Ignore the drama. Are you guys ready to get to work?"

Gathering around her, they nodded. The Breakout Crew, as Pierre would call them, spent a good hour in his basement conspiring to break Bug out of the shelter.

"Pierre, can you scrounge up a crowbar? Marina, Louisa, we need flashlights." Cellar Cat said. "I'm going to get Squirrelly. He'll know how to find the shelter. Tummy and Soda will come too. They can get into tight spots. I'll round them up and meet you at the swan gate in half an hour." "Hi ho." Cellar Cat yodeled to Squirrelly.

She had heard Bug use the greeting in times of distress. As she waited, she tried to remember what he told her about communicating with a squirrel. Chitter chatter, small words, and gestures. She hoped he would understand because more than anyone else, she needed Squirrelly's help. She didn't have to wait long. He perched himself above her on a branch, arms crossed.

"Chit, chit, chit, chat, chat, chat." she said, using hand gestures to re-create Bug's capture.

"Help! Please, please!" she said.

He tapped his foot, not understanding. She repeated the gestures again and finished with her digits up in prayer paws. An hour ago, she'd have thought pleading with a squirrel beneath her.

This time he nodded. He understood.

"Chit chat. Pound. Find?" she asked. She drew a building in the dirt with her nail. He nodded and was gone.

She scooted to the basement, collected the mice and was waiting by the gate when Squirrelly returned. Marina, Louisa, and Pierre arrived a second later. Marina and Pierre each held a flashlight in their mouths. Louisa balanced a crowbar between her teeth.

"Do you know where he is?" she asked the squirrel.

"Chit." He replied. He pointed far in the distance with one arm while bidding them to follow with the other.

Marching single file behind the squirrel, The Breakout Crew waded through belly-high puddles while being battered with rain. He led them away from their neighborhood toward the outer city. Tummy was balanced like a surfer between Cellar Cat's shoulder blades, and Soda clung spider-like to the back of her head. She didn't feel the discomfort of tiny mice nails digging into her skin because her only concern was the mission. She imagined Bug lonesome, cramped in a cell and sitting on a block of icy cement feeling lost and rejected. This drove her onward and she demanded that everyone pick up the pace.

Ten minutes later the crew faced a simple concrete building. The miserable trek did not compare to the defeat they felt in that moment. Cellar Cat bit her lower lip, suppressing a cry. The shelter was a fortress. Steel bars on every window. A steel gated door and a high chain-link fence with Impassable coils of barbed wire looped around the top were meant to keep animals in and intruders out. This is impossible, thought the cat.

"The good news is there's a closed sign on the door and no cars in the lot." Louisa said.

The outside lights were off and inside it was dark. One would think the building uninhabited if not for the occasional bark. Cellar Cat listened for Bug's low, slow howl amongst the bellows. She didn't hear it and that worried her. It had been several hours since he was taken. She willed herself not to imagine a stark dark room.

Overwhelmed and without a plan, a frustrated panic set in. Cellar Cat's reasoning skills shut down. They couldn't get Bug out and whatever was to happen or already happened to him was her fault. She hadn't noticed that he wasn't wearing his collar. She allowed him to dawdle rather than escorting him home immediately. She was responsible and now she had no plan to set him free. She was glad Bug wasn't there to see her fail. He always believed in her. Once again, she didn't measure up to his expectations.

"What dos we do?" squeaked Soda.

The plea snapped Cellar Cat back to problem-solving mode. A voice inside said, "Breathe." She dropped her head, took a breath and focused on the pitter-patter of the raindrops. Plunk, plunk, plunk. Calm washed over her. "Think."

the voice said. The panic evaporated and her thoughts were clear.

"Baby steps." she said aloud. The rest of the crew looked on, confused.

Since the fence was the first obstacle, she focused on that. The cat examined the area around it. One edge was bent, leaving a hole beneath it that led to the other side.

"Guys," she said to the mice. "see if you can squeeze through that hole and unlock the gate."

Tummy was too wide but Soda, with some squirming, made it through. She climbed the fence and unlocked the gate, but her arms weren't strong enough to lift the latch.
"Marina and Louisa, you're dogs. I bet you're both good diggers. Can you dig that hole big

enough for Squirrelly to get through? Pierre and I will hold the flashlights so you can see."

The big dogs got to work at once, and soon the hole was big enough for Squirrelly. It was tight and he had to work quickly before it filled with rainwater. On the other side, he shook off the mud. He vaulted from ground to gate in one swoop, landing on the latch with all his weight. The latch snapped up and the gate swung open. Everyone clapped. The crew bounded into the yard.

Cellar Cat immediately surveyed the building for any weak points.

An apple tree leaned into the side of the building. Squirrelly climbed it and investigated the structure from its knotty branches. He pointed to a window that had been left open by a crack.

"Can chit you chat fit through?" Cellar Cat called up, using her hands to simulate going in the window.

He shook his head no but tried to force it open more. It was jammed. "Is chat big chit enough for a mouse?" Cellar Cat asked. He frowned. "Dang." she said.

Louisa dropped the crowbar on the walkway at Cellar Cat's feet. Its clang startled her, but she got the point.

"Of course. I forgot about that."

"I can't reach it though. Too high." said Louisa.

"Ok." Cellar Cat pondered. Every problem has an solution if you just concentrate long enough.

"Marina, is it alright if Louisa stands on your back?"

Sour-faced, Marina agreed to position herself below the window and allow Louisa to climb her back. The boxer wrenched the crowbar under the crack in the windowsill. Though they were the right height to reach it, Louisa couldn't put enough pressure on the crowbar to pry the window open. Squirrelly communicated to Louisa to hold the pressure. He climbed higher in the apple tree, launched himself off the branch and landed full force on the crowbar. The window creaked but no more. The mice then ascended the mountain of animals, followed by Cellar Cat, and with their combined weight on the bar, the window lifted a fraction higher. It was enough for Squirrelly to wedge himself through. The mice popped in behind him, peeking their heads out for further instructions. "Unlock the door." said Cellar Cat.

"Buts we mights be too smalls to opens it." Soda said.

"It's a lever. Squirrelly can hang from it while we push it open from the outside. But be careful."

"Don't worry, we can do it. No problem." said Tummy.

The cat and dogs went to the padlocked metal gate that protected the front door. Cellar Cat wasted no time in sticking her sharpest nail inside. She dug around until the lock mechanism was released. Louisa gave a wink, pulled the padlock from the door and opened the gate.
They waited by the door until they heard the telltale click of the handle dropping. They pushed, there was a pop and the door swung open to reveal Squirrelly and the mice swinging

197

and grinning from the handle. As Marina was the first through the door, they plunked onto her back and jumped to the floor. She frowned at them.

The Breakout Crew found themselves in a dark hallway. The only light was a flickering exit sign.

"Stop!" Pierre said. "We need a lookout. I'd be honored to do it if there are no objections."

"Great idea. You stay. Bark if there's trouble." said Cellar Cat.

"Ok." He bowed and positioned himself between the front step and the door. He kept his chin rigid and his eyes sharp. "I shall take my duty seriously."

Everyone else shuffled on in the darkness.

"We have to be quick. In and out." Said Cellar Cat. She had the best night vision of the bunch but was confused by the choice of corridors. "Can anyone sniff out the kennel area?"

Marina stepped forward. "I'm still a good tracker."

"The best." Cellar Cat said, remembering how Marina had rescued Tummy from the alleyway. "Take the lead. Everyone else, silence."

The black dog snorted and sniffed, turning one direction then another before heading down a narrow passageway. They passed a purple door. Marina stopped and huffed. "I smell death."
She walked on, unruffled. The others gave it a wide berth as they passed. Cellar Cat wouldn't look at it at all, her only comfort being that Marina had not smelled Bug too. The hall ended at a wooden door with a thick window. The room within was dim. The light from the inner exit sign reflected off the metal cages. There were muffled whimpers as if someone were crying into a pillow.

"This is it." Marina said matter-of-factly.

Squirrelly crawled onto Louis's back and pulled down the door handle. It was unlocked. Cellar Cat let out a sigh of relief. They tip-toed into the room.

Once they had adjusted to the light, the crew took in the surroundings. It was a large room with rows of stacked cages and dog runs. Some were large enough for a St. Bernard, others Yorkie-sized. There was an adjacent room that was smaller and more crowded.

"We'll have to split up." Cellar Cat whispered, not wanting to alert the shelter dogs. "Marina and Louisa, you go left. Tummy, Soda, come with me. And Squirrelly-where's Squirrelly?"

Instead of waiting for instructions, the squirrel had climbed to the top of the cages, hopping from kennel to kennel, taking inventory. Most dogs were sleeping and the few that were awake were too wrapped up in their own misery to care what was going on around them.

"Shhhh." Cellar Cat reminded him.

The shelter was dismal and somber, just as Bug described it. Dingy kennels, sticky concrete floors and a foul smell. A place visibly voids of feeling yet brimming with sadness. Shame came over the cat. Back home she had all she ever wanted, but these dogs had nothing but bowls and a towel. No wonder Bug had been excited for a new life when he arrived in the basement only for her to insult him and make him feel unwanted. Why couldn't she have been kinder? Squirrelly, silently springing from above, gave the thumbs down as he went. Somewhere a metal bowl clanged on concrete and the room erupted in howls, yodels, and barks. Dogs who moments ago were in peaceful slumber now ran the length of their cages throwing themselves at the fence trying to get at the intruders.

Great! Now what? Cellar Cat thought. She beckoned the squirrel to her, motioning for him to collect the others. They needed to reconvene. Then, smack-dab in the middle of her chattering to Squirrelly, she heard it. A low, mournful wail. It was the sorriest thing she'd ever heard and she knew immediately that it was Bug.

She called out in the turmoil. "I'm coming, Bug!"

She and The Breakout Crew searched for the cry, making several wrong turns until they came to a stretch of small cages stacked five high. Squirrelly was already there, teetering on the topmost crate, pointing down into it. We found him, she said to herself. Bug was there.

She yelled his name but it was lost amongst the uproar. Louisa, fed up with the pandemonium, gave a sharp whistle. As quickly as it began, the noise ceased.

Squirrelly chattered something into the cage, and between the bars appeared a dirty white face and two dark eyes. The joy Cellar Cat felt at finding him dissipated at the sight of his sorry, defeated condition.

"Cellar Cat?" came a raspy voice. "Is that you?"

"It's all of us. We're here to save you."

"Everyone?" He coughed. "How?"

"No time to explain." She searched for a way to get him down. "Ideas, anyone?"

"We coulds climb up there to opens his cage."

"Thanks, Soda, but Squirrelly can do that. I mean how do we get him down?"

The shelter dogs were now transfixed by the events and called out suggestions, like "Climb on each other to make a stack." To which Louisa replied, "He's not limber enough to climb down from that." Another yelled, "push the cage over," to which Cellar Cat replied, "Yeah, if we want to carry him home on a stretcher."

"I know. We get a blanket. We each hold a side and he jump." said Pierre.

"What are you doing? You're supposed to be guarding the door." said Marina.

"I heard a commotion. Squirrelly can guard it now. I'll hold the blanket with my strong jaw." He clamped his teeth to prove his point.

"I saw a pile of blankets and bedding on a shelf on the way in." Said the cat. The squirrel opened Bug's cage door, gave a salute and was gone."I don't know. It's risky. Bug is solid. What if he falls through?"

"We could put a bed underneath just in case." squeaked Tummy.

She scratched her chin. "That might work." It wasn't a sure thing, but time was running out.

204

Morning was approaching and a decision had to be made.

"What's going on down there?" Bug asked, somewhat alarmed.

"Just be patient. I'll let you know what to do."

Pierre retrieved the strongest blanket he could find while Louisa dragged two padded beds over. She anticipated where he'd fall and placed them there. Meanwhile, the mice climbed up the tower of crates to comfort Bug. Once at the top, they bombarded him with hugs and kisses.

"Love you, Buggy Pops!" they sang.

Although excited to see them, his attentions were not far from the activity below.

"What now?" he yelled down.

There was no answer because each canine and cat held a corner of the blanket in their teeth.

"Ya gotta jumps." Soda said.

"Oh no. No, no, no. Sorry, can't. Too far."
"Ya gots to, Pops." she pleaded.

"You can do it." Said Tummy. "We believe in you. Everyone believes in you."

"That's nice, little ones but I don't like heights."

Cellar Cat heard him and dropped her end of the blanket.

"Some wise dog once told me to take some breaths, feel the fear fully, then let it pass. Take baby steps if you have to, but jump! We're not leaving without you. If you don't, come sunrise, we'll all be in cages."

She picked up the blanket and resumed her stance. They each held a corner as taut as could be.

Bug nodded. He took a multitude of deep inhales and exhales. When panic welled up inside him, he let them pass through.

He managed the small fear that remained by focusing on the task at hand.

"I'm going for it." he said.

"Do it, Pops!" the mice hollered. Shelter dogs, watching, spoke words of encouragement.

Bug said "It's now or never. "

He took one more inhale and kicked his feet clear of the cage. He plummeted toward the concrete. He closed his eyes. Suddenly, the blanket gave way beneath him. He bounced up off the springy beds below and back into the blanket. The fabric collapsed around him. When he opened his eyes, he was greeted by his friends faves looking down at him.

The mice scrambled to the floor and smothered him again. Bug, overwhelmed by the love, beamed at his friends. He saved a special wink for his Cellar Cat.

"Thanks guys. I don't—"

"Look."

Pierre was pointing toward the exit. Squirrelly was there chittering away excitedly.

"He says it's dawn." Louisa said. "The shelter opens soon. We need to go."

The Breakout Crew headed toward the exit. Bug stopped at the purple door on the way out.

"Don't worry about that." Cellar Cat said with confidence. "You're never coming back here or to any other shelter for that matter. I told you before—I won't leave you."
She bumped his shoulder. The two shared a laugh and walked on.

Though the drizzle and early morning fog made the city appear dreary, the walk home was full of charged excitement. The group reveled in the night's events and celebrated each other's bravery. Squirrelly, chattering away to Louisa while riding on her back, would occasionally slap her side whilst chortling. Tummy snored on

Pierre's head as the Frenchie complimented Marina on her tracking skills. She, in turn, praised his decision-making skills and ability to take direction. While their friends talked, Cellar Cat and Bug dropped behind. He was aglow, marveling at the cold rain, wet sidewalks, gray mist, and the sounds of his friends' laughter. Soda was stretched out on his back with her head resting on her paws. Intermittently, the mouse reached out toward Cellar Cat to hug her. The cat would return the gesture.

"Are you ok? Was it terrible? Were they mean to you?" she asked.

He frowned. "I don't recall. All that matters is that you came to my rescue." Joy spread across his face. "No one has ever done anything like that for me."

"Aunty Cellar organized its all, Pops." Soda said sleepily. "She evens talked with Squirrellys and wasn't means about it."

"Really?" Bug asked. "You've come such a long way."
"Naw. Everyone helped. It was a group effort." Said the cat.

"That's true." said Marina.

Everyone had stopped and were surrounding them. They were home.
"No one could bear the thought of you in that horrible place." Said Louisa.

"You're a good one." said Pierre, handing a limp Tummy off to Cellar Cat, who placed him beside Soda on Bug's back. "Can't wait for the next adventure with you all." the bulldog called, prancing off to house.

Marina walked over to Bug and placed her nose on his. "Until we meet again, take care, gentle soul."

Louisa waved before she and Marina bounded for their yard. Bug stood motionless, sniffling for a minute or two then rejoining Cellar Cat and Squirrelly.

The sun rose as they crossed the street. Squirrelly leapt ahead, climbed his tree in a neighboring yard and vanished into its branches.

"Thank you." Bug croaked. "I forgot his name."

Cellar Cat knew his mind was tiring; the day had taken its toll. No words were exchanged from the backyard to the basement. The room was warm and inviting. Bug dropped into his bed. The cat picked the mice off his back and returned them to their beds. While tucking Soda in, the mouse kissed her on the cheek. Cellar Cat blushed. Why hadn't she liked mice?

She dragged herself to the sofa, ready to sleep the day away. The cushiony material enveloped her. She couldn't remember ever being so snug and secure. Bug was nestled in his bed, eyes closed, mouth slightly upturned. She watched him thoughtfully.

Climbing down from her comfy sofa, she padded over to the old dog, cleared her throat and curled up next to him.

"Cellar Cat, I decided something." The dog yawned.

"Oh yeah? What's that?"

"You're my being."

"Huh?"

His words seemed muddled, and she wondered if he was confused again.

"What I mean is, you're my best friend. The greatest friend I've ever had, if that makes any sense." His eyes remained closed. "It's ok if you don't feel the same. I just wanted to tell you."

She wasn't sure how to respond. Maybe something sarcastic to lighten the mood. No, she was too old for such childish talk. Instead, she looked up at Bug's sweet face, stretched one long arm over his floppy ear, patted the crown of his head three times, and said,

"You're right, Bug. We are best buds. Ditto on the other stuff too."

She put her head on his shoulder and began purring. "Bff's?" he said softly. "Baby steps, Bug." She snuggled up closer. "Baby steps."

TEMPLETON ESQUIRE

Frigid winds blew wreaths of snow past the basement window. Inside it was toasty. Much had changed over the years. At the far end of the room, where Tummy's boxed home used to be, was a roaring wood stove. The wallpaper had been stripped and painted over in eggshell white. The doughy sofa was replaced with a stiff loveseat and the high-back chairs were gone. All storage boxes and containers were stored in the attic. Below Cellar Cat's window was a crafting corner consisting of a wide desk, a sewing machine, swivel chair and sewing baskets. Long ornate bookshelves full of crafting books and supplies were the main focus of the room. The stairs were updated and carpeted and a closet was built beneath the staircase. The dilapidated bureau Soda once used as a bedroom had been refurbished and painted an ocean green by the owner. One of her many projects since retirement.

Cellar Cat, who's coat had gone gray, had long since refused to sleep on the hard couch. You could find her tucked beneath a frayed green blanket atop a ragged dog bed. Her hearing was bad and her sight was poor.

Other than the slight shake of the icy window sills and the crackling fire, all was quiet. The cat was snoring when the basement door opened. The sound barely registered. The woman often spent time in the basement so the cat readjusted her tail and went back to sleep.

"Oh, Cellar dear?" the woman said.

Cellar Cat yawned, stretched and tunneled her head out from under her blanket. The owner stood above her holding a small object. The cat's eyesight was poor and she thought it was an orange.

"Wooket the wittle sweetheart." said the woman, laying the thing on the new wood floor beside the dog bed. An orange tabby kitten with bright blue eyes slid to and fro on the slippery surface. When it saw Cellar Cat it hissed.

"Awwww, what a screwy girl." Said the owner.

She stooped down to pet Cellar Cat. "Poor baby lost her mama, just like you."

She picked up the kitten up and kissed its face. "Don't worry, Cellar Cat will take good care of you." After a few more smooches, she again placed the kitten down beside the bed. It hissed again.

The owner grabbed a book from the bookshelf and walked upstairs.

"Watch it, lady, I bite." the kitten said. It arched its back while crab-walking around the old cat.

Cellar Cat chuckled and the kitten relaxed. "What's your name, little monster?"
The kitten scowled. "Templeton Esquire."
A long name for a tiny being.

"What's the matter? You don't like your name?"

"Well," said the orange tabby. "it's just—I'm not a boy. Because most orange cats are boys, the owner thought it would be funny to give me a boy's name."
"Shall I call you something different, then?"

"No."

"Templeton Esquire it is, then. It's a fine name." The warm glow from the wood stove reflected on the elder cat's face. "So, what do you want to do, little one? Nap? Play? There are toys in that basket over there. I don't play anymore, so you'll have to sift through to find newer ones."

Templeton skated over to the wooden basket. Rummaging through it, she ignored the newer toys and pulled out pieces that interested her. A mouse toy, a pocket-sized stuffed bunny, and a worry doll she dug up from the bottom. She laid them all out on the floor trying to decide which to play with when she noticed something shiny under Cellar Cat's blanket. She batted at it and dragged the edge out with her teeth.

"No dear, you may have anything in that basket, but this is not a toy. It's too precious."

"What is it?"

Cellar Cat pulled a shabby blue collar out from under the blanket.

"Ehhh. It's just a crappy old dog collar."

"That may be," said Cellar Cat. She picked it up and dangled it on the tip of her nail "but this crappy collar," she continued, pulling it close to her chest, "belonged to the kindest, most loving dog I ever knew."

"Ok, ok. Sorry. Dramatic much? Yeesh."

"Sometimes old and worn items have more value than shiny new ones. The memories they hold make them precious." Cellar Cat sighed. There was a brief silence, as if she were reliving a particular moment. "You'll learn that someday." The kitten wrinkled her nose. "Come on, let's get you settled. Snack, play, bath then nap. How's that sound?"

"You had me at snack. A bath, though?" Templeton frowned.

"Yup. 'Fraid so, little monster. And if you don't sit still for it, there's an elderly squirrel who'd be happy to help me. He's a
bit   unpredictable   and   a   whole   lotta temperamental."

"Dang."

Cellar Cat pointed to the stairs. The kitten's frown turned devilish.
"Woohoo, last one to the top is a cockroach!"
Templeton Esquire darted up the stairs. The aged cat took each step carefully. At the last one, she turned and gazed fondly out the window at a snow-covered wooden cross. Resting below the white powder were heaps of mementos left by long ago friends including pebbles, crystals, acorn shells, and a cigar box. A gold plaque at the center of the cross was engraved with a silver dog paw print and shiny bronze lettering that read:

"In our hearts forever."

Scratched into the bottom of the cross and only legible to animals were these words:

HERE LIES BUG A GOOD BOY

Cellar Cat bowed and said "I remember everything you taught me, Bug. I got this." She turned and silently vanished through the door flap.

Made in United States
North Haven, CT
23 April 2024

51684151R00124